Cinematherapy

GOES TO THE OSCARS

ALSO BY NANCY PESKE AND BEVERLY WEST:

Cinematherapy for the Soul: The Girl's Guide to Finding Inspiration, One Movie at a Time

Cinematherapy for Lovers: The Girl's Guide to Finding True Love, One Movie at a Time

Advanced Cinematherapy: The Girl's Guide to Finding Happiness, One Movie at a Time

Bibliotherapy: The Girl's Guide to Books for Every Phase of Our Lives

Cinematherapy: The Girl's Guide to Movies for Every Mood

Frankly Scarlett, I *Do* Give a Damn! Classic Romances Retold

AND UNDER THE PSEUDONYM LEE WARD SHORE:

How to Satisfy a Woman Every Time on Five Dollars a Day

Meditations for Men Who Do Next to Nothing (and Would Like to Do Even Less)

Cinematherapy

GOES TO THE OSCARS

The Girl's Guide to the Best Movie Medicine Ever Made

by NANCY PESKE and BEVERLY WEST

UNIVERSE

First published in the United States of America in 2004

by UNIVERSE PUBLISHING

A Division of Rizzoli International Publications, Inc.

300 Park Avenue South

New York, NY 10010

www.rizzoliusa.com

2004 2005 2006 2007/ 10 9 8 7 6 5 4 3 2 1

Printed in the United States of America

Design by Headcase Design • www.headcasedesign.com

ISBN: 0-7893-1193-3

Library of Congress Catalog Control Number: 2004113998

TO NEW BEGINNINGS
AND HAPPY ENDINGS

ACKNOWLEDGMENTS

Bev and Nancy would like to thank the two newlyweds in our life: our editor Kathleen Jayes, for her loyalty and constancy, even in the midst of wedding plans, and our agent Neeti Madan, who has lent her creativity and insight to this series from its beginning, and to whom we owe a great debt of gratitude for her years of careful stewardship. We would also like to thank our tireless publicist Pamela Sommers, and Maurice Vellekoop for bringing these pages into a new dimension with his inspiring illustrations.

Bev would like to thank all of the timeless classics in her life, including: Ellen Rees, David Olds, Joe Kolker, Kim Doi, Pam Conway, Deborah Jean Baynes, Richard Haslow, Josh Kent, Kristen Kreft, Tom Pennacchini, and especially Jason Bergund, my unexpected happily ever after.

Nancy would like to thank all the folks who help her to live happily ever after, but especially George and Dante, Richard and Carol, Mom and Dad, Lindsey, Hellie, and Tony & Kerry.

CONTENTS

INTRODUCTION

....

Finally, a guide to the Oscars that acknowledges what many of us have known for years—the Academy Awards are a lot more than just an awards show, they're a slice of American history, and Oscar movies are more than entertainment, they're group therapy that helped us as a country to examine our conflicts, grieve over our losses, celebrate our successes, and carry on through adversity.

Cinematherapy Goes to the Oscars takes a unique look at Oscar history and what it says about us as a nation, examining what the Oscar-winning movies in each decade offered to us as individuals, and as a country. These are the films that helped us work through our collective anxiety, get to the bottom of our father issues, and look under the surface to what was really going on. They made us laugh, cry, reflect, and find the courage to face our challenges. Whatever the zeitgeist, moviemakers found ways to bring it to life on the screen, and helped us connect to one another through good times, bad times, and downright absurd times.

- On the verge of your nineteenth nervous breakdown? Watch one of Oscar 2000s Antianxiety Movies like *Finding Nemo*, and breathe a little easier.

- Caught in the rainstorm of life without an umbrella? Watch one of Oscar 1980s Don't Worry, Be . . . in Denial Movies like *Rain Man*, and let the sun shine.

- Dad driving you nuts? Watch an Oscar 1970s My Heart Belongs to Daddy Movie like *Paper Moon*, and heal the rift.

We've also included lots of fun sidebars like Bev's Oscar Bash, with tips and recipes for throwing an award-winning Oscar party; Oops! Did I Say That Out Loud?: Famous and Infamous Quotes from Oscar Winners; and What Were They Thinking?, featuring movies that Oscar shut out or fawned over, much to our bafflement.

And of course, we take a look at the classic Academy Awards moments featuring Oscar's biggest stars—those bedazzled, big-screen emblems of the best and the worst in ourselves, only thinner and with better upper body development, who every year make their way down that legendary red carpet, and, if we're lucky, trip over their hem and prove that even the most celebrated among us have trouble walking in stilettos.

Whether it was an era of war or peace, prosperity or poverty, cultural upheaval or suburban complacency, the movies that dominated the Academy Awards spoke to the hearts of audiences who wanted to see their hopes, fears, and values reflected on screen, whether played out in high drama or in romantic comedy. And while some of the Academy's picks stand the test of time better than others, these seventy-five-plus years' worth of movies represent an impressive pharmacy of Cinematherapeutic elixirs and balms for audiences today. Whether they swept the awards or won only one of their many nominations, the films in *Cinematherapy Goes to the Oscars* all reassure us that no matter what we're going through, we're not alone, and that even when all looks bleak, we can have faith that ultimately the best in human nature will triumph.

Chapter One

OSCAR IN THE 2000s

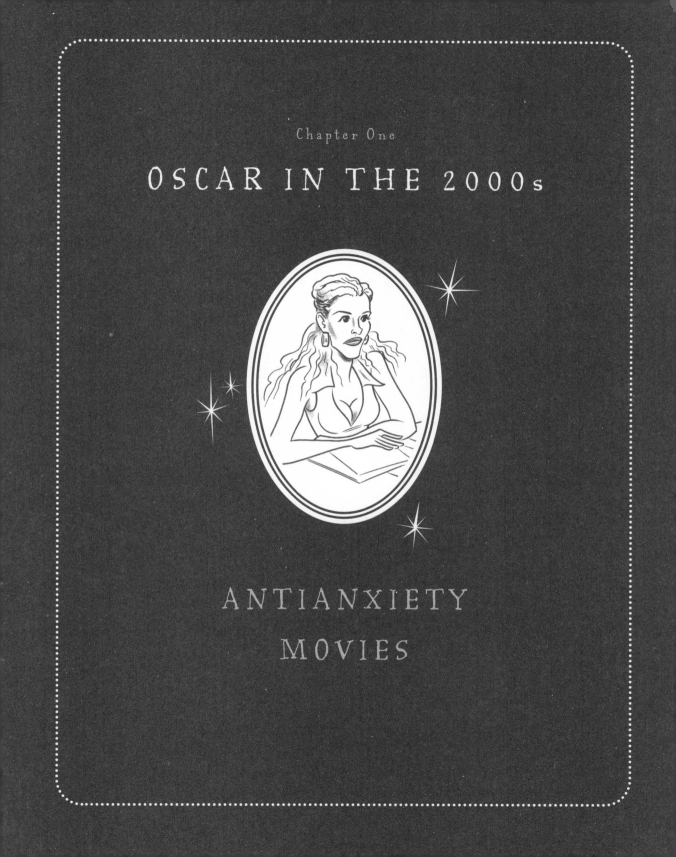

ANTIANXIETY

MOVIES

The new-millennium Oscars are dominated by Antianxiety Movies, featuring heroes and heroines who have to develop nerves of steel—and in most instances really great pecs and abs—to brave the storm. Movies in this decade take on the monsters of the mind, corporate corruption, alcoholism, domestic violence, prejudice, and even the perverse pleasures of a crumbling and decadent empire or the dungeons of ancient Rome. And somehow, from the ashes, they rise up and find redemption. Along the way, these Antianxiety heroes and heroines learn the hard lessons of the storm: that in helping one another we help ourselves; that it's never a good idea to deny reality, particularly when automatic weapons, chariots, or antidepressants are concerned; and that with courage, faith, a little media savvy, and a reliable broad sword, you can rebuild Rome. So when you're feeling jumpy, turn the lights down low, throw some popcorn in a bowl, and calm down with a new-millennium Antianxiety Movie. And remember that you don't have to be afraid of the dark.

ERIN BROCKOVICH (2000)

STARS ....Julia Roberts, Albert Finney, Aaron Eckhart, Marg Helgenberger

DIRECTOR..Steven Soderbergh

WRITER...Susannah Grant

ACADEMY AWARDS ....Best Actress, plus four nominations, including Best Picture

In the year 2000, we all still believed in tech stocks, the global village, and the integrity of our election process, so it's no wonder that we embraced a movie about a well-endowed but under-employed single mom who takes on a corporate Goliath and wins. Julia Roberts, in her America's Sweetheart years, stars as the feisty Erin Brockovich, whose cleavage became a national metaphor for the power of a woman's scorn. Down on her heels, and with three mouths to feed, Erin forces her own personal injury lawyer, Ed Masry (Albert Finney), to give her a job. She is assigned to the file room, and amid the dust and dead letters, discovers her personal crusade to take down a power company that has poisoned an entire town and redeem herself. Along the way, she strikes a blow for single moms, the working man, and fading beauty queens with plunging necklines everywhere. So if you've been feeling suffocated by the turtleneck of your life, and afraid of what life has in store for you, let *Erin Brockovich* reassure you with the optimistic spirit of Oscar 2000, when cinematic cleavage was celebrated rather than litigated, and a door closing always meant that a better one was opening, just over the next bump in the road.

GO AHEAD, MAKE MY DAY

"Look I don't know shit about shit but I know right from wrong!"

"So tell me something Scott—does PG&E pay you to cover their ass, or do you just do it out of the kindness of your heart?"

ALL QUOTES FROM JULIA ROBERTS
AS ERIN BROCKOVICH IN *ERIN BROCKOVICH*

FINDING NEMO (2003)

STARS ....Albert Brooks, Ellen DeGeneres, Alexander Gould, Elizabeth Perkins

DIRECTORS ....Andrew Stanton, Lee Unkrich

WRITERS ....Andrew Stanton, Bob Peterson, David Reynolds

ACADEMY AWARDS ....Best Animated Feature Film, plus three nominations

In the 2000s, the tempestuous world offers us plenty of opportunities to let anxiety get the better of us. But—as this movie about an overly attached father shows—when we let that happen, we can end up creating the very problems we fear most.

Marlin (Albert Brooks), a clownfish in the coral reefs off Australia, has a good excuse for not letting his son, Nemo (Alexander Gould), stretch his wings—er, fins. Ever since the day a barracuda appeared at the sea anemone home of Marlin and his wife Coral (Elizabeth Perkins) and swallowed up Coral and all her eggs, Marlin has had only Nemo at his side. Nemo also ended up with one fin that's slightly undersized, which gives his father another reason for kvetching every time the little fish dares to swim out of reach. Frustrated by his father's lack of faith in him, a rebellious Nemo takes an extra-long swim one day, and is captured and plopped in an aquarium in some dentist's office.

While the despairing Marlin swims frantically toward the wake of the boat that carried away his son, he meets a happy-go-lucky fish named Dory (Ellen DeGeneres), who takes him on a journey. Marlin learns valuable lessons—like, how sometimes you have to go with the flow (of the jet stream, that is), how sometimes you've got to go down into the belly of the beast and trust that you'll escape, and how sometimes when you're most confused, afraid, and lost, you just have to keep swimming, swimming, swimming.

When you've been getting signals that you need to back up and back off a bit, pop in *Finding Nemo* and ride the wave back to serenity and acceptance.

HANG TEN, DUDE

CRUSH THE SEA TURTLE (ANDREW STANTON): You know, you leave them on the beach to hatch on their own . . . and coo-coo-cachoo, they find their way back to the big old blue.

MARLIN THE CLOWNFISH (ALBERT BROOKS): Wow. How do you know when they're ready?

CRUSH THE SEA TURTLE: You don't really, you know? Like when they know, you'll know, ya know?

FROM FINDING NEMO

DORY (ELLEN DEGENERES): Hey there, Mr. Grumpy Gills. When life gets you down, do you wanna know what you've gotta do?

Marlin (Albert Brooks): No, I don't wanna know.

DORY (SINGING): Just keep swimming. Just keep swimming. Just keep swimming, swimming, swimming. What do we do? We swim, swim.

FROM FINDING NEMO

LOST IN TRANSLATION (2003)

STARS..**Bill Murray, Scarlett Johansson**

DIRECTOR AND WRITER..**Sofia Coppola**

ACADEMY AWARDS......................................**Best Screenplay, plus three nominations**

. . . .

The relationship between two unlikely soul mates adrift in an unfamiliar place provides a cinematic opportunity for us all to take a deep breath and reassure ourselves that when the student is ready, the teacher appears.

Bill Murray stars as Bob Harris, an aging matinee idol who is in Tokyo for a few days to film a whiskey commercial for which he will make way too much money and gain not nearly enough personal satisfaction. Haunted by guilt over his fractured relationship with his family and himself, he drifts through the four-star luxury accommodations of his self-imposed emotional exile with a deadpan that is virtually impenetrable. And then Bob bumps into Charlotte (Scarlett Johansson), a fellow emotional expatriate adrift in a kingdom of clutter, whose husband has forgotten her almost as completely as she has forgotten herself. What begins as tentative chitchat between two fellow insomniacs blossoms into a brief but life-transforming communion between two lost souls who find themselves by finding each other, and a reassuring reminder for us all that there is no loneliness or isolation so profound that we can't find a human connection, so long as we're willing to open our hearts and receive the current.

I'D RATHER HAVE A BOTTLE
IN FRONT OF ME

CHARLOTTE (SCARLETT JOHANSSON): So, what are you doing here?
BOB (BILL MURRAY): Uh, a couple of things. Taking a break from my wife,
forgetting my son's birthday. And, uh, getting paid two million dollars
to endorse a whiskey when I could be doing a play somewhere.
CHARLOTTE: Oh.
BOB: But the good news is, the whiskey works.
FROM *LOST IN TRANSLATION*

"You want more mysterious? I'll just try and think where the hell's the whiskey."

BILL MURRAY

AS BOB HARRIS IN *LOST IN TRANSLATION*

WHAT WERE THEY THINKING?

SEABISCUIT (2003)

STARS ....Jeff Bridges, Tobey Maguire

DIRECTOR ....Gary Ross

WRITER ....Gary Ross, based on the book by Laura Hillenbrand

ACADEMY AWARDS ....seven nominations, including Best Picture; no wins

How could Oscar fawn all over *Lord of the Rings* and snub this movie about a Depression-era racehorse who served as a metaphor for triumph over adversity? Like a nice warm cup of tea on a rainy afternoon, *Seabiscuit* promises that we too can beat the odds and race across the finish line to victory.

Despite his Thoroughbred breeding, Seabiscuit himself was written off as not having any racing potential because he was too small and lacking in competitive spirit, and he blew his first few races. Ah, but Charles Howard (Jeff Bridges) thought he was the little engine that could, so he bought him, set him up with a trainer (Chris Cooper) who could tweak the performance of any old paint, and assigned him a too-tall jockey named Red Pollard (Tobey Maguire), who refused to quit even when his race-loss record rivaled his drunken-binge-in-Tijuana record. Newspapers and radio announcers said Seabiscuit and Pollard were hopeless, but Howard believed that prosperity and recovery were just around the corner, so he ignored the naysayers and persevered.

This true tale from the 1930s had a second life as a magazine article, a third as a book, a fourth as a movie, and a fifth as a human interest story about the book's author, who battled crippling chronic fatigue syndrome and vertigo to finish her manuscript—talk about a can-do story with legs. Watch this one when you need a little tap on the flank to encourage you to keep on keepin' on, despite your fear that you don't have what it takes.

Documentarians offer us stories that are both entertaining and informative, but they often choose politically or emotionally charged subject matter, and they don't necessarily tell us the other side of the story. Thus, their films often attract controversy—or at least some griping from the folks who didn't get interviewed. The Oscar-winning documentaries of the new millennium are no exception.

These films remind us, each in its own way, that it can be hard to face our fears, but hiding from them just results in problems so deeply destructive that they simply demand to be exposed via their own documentary. So when you're in the mood to wake up, deal with reality, and start working on solutions instead of feeding your anxiety, check out these eye-opening films and start asking the hard questions.

THE FOG OF WAR:
ELEVEN LESSONS FROM THE LIFE
OF ROBERT S. McNAMARA (2003)

DIRECTOR .... Errol Morris

PRODUCER .... Michael Williams

ACADEMY AWARDS .... Best Documentary, Feature

When a man reaches a certain age, it's only natural for him to reflect on the mistakes he's made and the lessons he's learned. Of course, when the mistakes one has made resulted in the horrific and unnecessary deaths of thousands of soldiers and civilians, it can be a tad difficult to maintain an unemotional demeanor. But in this straight-talking documentary, octogenarian Robert S. McNamara sure does his best to keep his eyes dry while sticking to cold facts and hard logic.

McNamara, a clearly brilliant man who was the U.S. secretary of defense under Kennedy and Johnson during the Vietnam War era, details his triumphs and tribulations with an equal amount of honesty. He can laugh off personal questions about his notorious arrogance. But when the interviewer coaxes him to indulge in a mea culpa about promising the American public that the tide was turning over there in Southeast Asia, really it was, when actually he and LBJ were clueless about what to do, McNamara quickly becomes taciturn and mysterious, muttering something about how complicated it all was. Oh, okay then.

This documentary offers not only a fascinating insight into a painful chapter of America's past but a powerful portrayal of that male attitude of the gray-flannel-suit generation that allows only so much mucking about in difficult, messy emotions before moving on to more comfortable intellectual territory.

BOWLING FOR COLUMBINE (2002)

DIRECTOR AND WRITER ....Michael Moore

PRODUCER ....Michael Donovan

ACADEMY AWARDS ....Best Documentary, Feature

Americans watched in horror as the massacre at suburban Colorado's Columbine High School unfolded on that awful day, and the sheer ordinariness of the school and the two students turned killers—who casually spent the morning bowling before their blaze of destruction—shook us to our very core, causing us to ask ourselves, how did this happen? And how can we prevent it from happening again? In this scintillating documentary, which invokes a gamut of emotions from anger to frustration, amusement, and compassion, filmmaker Michael Moore doesn't allow for easy finger-pointing. He quickly squelches the usual theories about the roots of violence and instead dares us to look more deeply at our fears, which, left unexplored, feed upon themselves until one day we're dressed in camouflage and talking about protecting ourselves from some unseen enemy as our two-year-old toddles around fingering the home arsenal. Moore's documentary is as bracing as a grande java, forcing us to wake up and smell the coffee already.

"You don't need no gun control. You know what you need? Bullet control.
I think all bullets should cost $5,000. You know why?
If a bullet cost $5,000, there'd be no more innocent bystanders."

CHRIS ROCK
IN *BOWLING FOR COLUMBINE*

MURDER ON A
SUNDAY MORNING (2001)

DIRECTOR .... Jean-Xavier de Lestrade

PRODUCER .... Denis Poncet

ACADEMY AWARDS .... Best Documentary, Feature

Sometimes it takes an outsider—in this case, a French filmmaker—to expose the dark undertow of racism we'd prefer to believe doesn't exist in our American culture. This documentary follows the trial of a young African American male (Brenton Butler) accused of the senseless and brutal killing of a white American tourist named Mary Stephens one sunny Sunday morning in Jacksonville, Florida.

Given the circumstances of the arrest, it seems that the kid's crime might best be described as "walking while black." Any American who values justice should have at least a slightly queasy feeling in his or her stomach at learning the details of this racially charged case. Sure, we are privy to some huge problems with the prosecution's claims—from an obviously coerced confession, to an eyewitness who missed a humongous logo on a T-shirt from the distance of three feet in broad daylight, and a complete lack of anything resembling an actual investigation. But can justice prevail?

Enter defense attorney Patrick McGuiness, a stocky Irishman who just loves a good fight and takes it personally when cops don't do their jobs, and we're reminded that if we all would have the courage to face facts and do our jobs properly, and if everyone would just respect the system by working with it instead of against it, we Americans might actually succeed in discovering the truth and overcoming the forces of fear and corruption.

INTO THE ARMS OF STRANGERS: STORIES OF THE KINDERTRANSPORT (2000)

DIRECTOR AND WRITER ....Mark John Harris

PRODUCER ....Deborah Oppenheimer

ACADEMY AWARDS ....Best Documentary, Feature

At the beginning of World War II, terrified for the safety of their children but unable to flee Europe for various reasons, many German, Austrian, and Czechoslovakian Jewish parents made the painful decision to send their kids to England to be cared for by strangers for the duration. This movie explores the complex emotional landscape created by the Kindertransport project, which doled out children to British households: some warm and loving, others cold and distant, and most colored by that British custom of carrying on, cheerio, without talking about painful matters. Confused by what was going on, afraid to let on in letters to their parents just how lonely and sad they were, the children ultimately had to find their own way to process this extraordinary experience, reminding us all that frank conversation and acknowledgment of our fears can go a long way toward fostering feelings of security.

MYSTIC RIVER (2003)

STARS .... Sean Penn, Tim Robbins, Kevin Bacon, Laurence Fishburne,
.... Marcia Gay Harden, Laura Linney, Emmy Rossum

DIRECTOR .... Clint Eastwood

WRITER .... Brian Helgeland, based on the novel by Dennis Lehane

ACADEMY AWARDS .... Best Actor (Sean Penn), Best Supporting Actor (Tim Robbins),
.... plus four nominations, including Best Picture

After a terribly destructive storm, it can be tempting to simply move on and try not think about it anymore. But as this movie about three men who never quite processed the tragedy that befell one of them in their youth goes to show, it's not such a good idea to repress the flood of emotions, because some day that leaky dike will burst.

By a twist of fate, Dave Boyle (Tim Robbins) was kidnapped and molested as a child while two buddies who were with him, Jimmy (Sean Penn) and Sean (Kevin Bacon), escaped harm. Well, at least that's what everyone in their peeling-paint-and-broken-linoleum South Side Boston neighborhood wanted to believe, so no one ever discussed what happened or how it affected all three boys. Now that they're adults, however, their paths intertwine again when Jimmy's daughter (Emmy Rossum) goes missing. Sean, now a police detective, is called in to head the investigation, and Dave wanders about making mysterious comments that have even his wife (Marcia Gay Harden) harboring suspicions. Well, partly it's because of her husband's evasiveness, partly it's that faraway look in his eye, and partly it's because he came back with bruises and blood all over his clothes the night Jimmy's daughter disappeared. Yep, there are a lot of questions to be answered, threads to be untangled, and old wounds to be reopened, but will these men have the courage to not give in to fear, rage, and revenge?

When you're tempted to seek shelter in the happy, sunny land of denial, watch *Mystic River* and brace yourself for a compelling cautionary tale about the perils of squelching painful emotions, pretending everything's just dandy, and letting others imagine what could be going through your mind.

BEV'S OSCAR BASH

If you've got the beautiful people coming over to your villa, whet your whistle in true Hollywood style with this Tinseltowntini, guaranteed to wow the glitterati.

THE TINSELTOWNTINI
(serves one Oscar winner and one nominee)

HERE'S WHAT YOU'LL NEED:
- 2 ounces Goldschlagger
- 3 ounces vanilla vodka
- 2 ounces apple juice
- 1 twist of lemon

HERE'S HOW YOU DO IT:
Pour everything into a cocktail shaker filled with ice, shake vigorously, and strain into chilled martini glasses. Garnish with a twist, which will contrast fetchingly with the gold flakes glittering amid the flaxen confluences of your 18-karat martini.

WARNING LABEL: Before hitting the red carpet after a couple of these martinis, it's advisable to look in a mirror and make sure you haven't got any gold stuck in your teeth or a lampshade on your head.

CHICAGO (2002)

STARS ....Renée Zellweger, Catherine Zeta-Jones, Richard Gere,
....Queen Latifah, John C. Reilly

DIRECTOR ....Rob Marshall

WRITER ....Bill Condon, based on the play by Maurine Dallas Watkins,
....based on the musical by Bob Fosse

ACADEMY AWARDS ....Best Picture, Best Supporting Actress (Catherine Zeta-Jones),
....Best Costume Design, plus three more awards and seven nominations

This romp through the City of Sin and Gin in the jazz age had us all doing Fosse arms in the face of disaster, and ordering one for the road. Catherine Zeta-Jones and Renée Zellweger star as Velma Kelly and Roxie Hart, two of the baddest bad girls in a big bad town who get away with murder and go on to star in their fifteen minutes of fame without suffering a moment's fear, regret, or even a well-deserved hangover. Even when the long arm of the law does come knocking, Velma and Roxie elude Judgment Day once more with the help of rainmaker Billy Flynn (Richard Gere). Billy is a hotshot attorney with a gift for fancy footwork who tap-dances his way across the dividing line between good and evil without missing a single kick-ball-change. Ultimately, Billy Flynn and Bob Fosse's high-stepping hurricane of ill repute lands us in a different kind of Oz, where the only morality is entertainment, and bad ratings are punishable by death.

In the first years of a new millennium characterized by uncertainty, an obsession with celebrity, and a pervasive fear of the unknown, it is no wonder that we were fascinated by a movie that reassured us that when the going gets tough, the tough find a whoopee spot with a reliable gin mill and a good floor show and wait out the storm. And if that doesn't work, there's always Queen Latifah.

THERE'S NO BUSINESS
LIKE SHOW BUSINESS

"Oooh, the audience loves me...and I love them.
And they love me for loving them and I love them for loving me.
And we love each other. And that's because none of us got enough
love in our childhood. And that's showbiz, kid."

RENÉE ZELLWEGER
AS ROXIE HART IN *CHICAGO*

SHREK (2001)

STARS .... Mike Myers, Eddie Murphy, Cameron Diaz, John Lithgow

DIRECTORS .... Andrew Adamson, Vicky Jenson

WRITERS .... Ted Elliott, Terry Rossio, Joe Stillman, Roger S. H. Schulman, et al.,
.... based on the book by William Steig

ACADEMY AWARDS .... Best Full-Length Animated Feature Film, plus one nomination

As we face the new millennium, and we still haven't overcome bigotry or sexism, it's nice to revise our culture's mythologies to create a comforting fairy-tale world we can all take shelter in—a world where even an ogre has a shot at true love, and a princess doesn't have to be supermodel-pretty to find her soul mate.

Turning upside down the usual fairy-tale rules, *Shrek* presents us with a hero who isn't blessed with leading-man looks. In fact, he bathes in slime and lives in a smelly swamp, but Shrek (Mike Myers), ogre that he is, accepts that about himself. However, after years of having frightened locals spread stories about him, Shrek has given up believing that his way of living could ever be fine with anyone else. Then one day, a donkey (Eddie Murphy), who also defies the rules of convention—he can actually talk—shows up in Shrek's neck of the woods, and this unlikely pair embark on a quest that leads them to realize that love transcends beauty, open heartedness triumphs over fear and prejudice, and full-length feature animated films don't have to be preschool-wholesome, or set to Elton John/Tim Rice ballads.

When you're in the mood to get away from the torrent of formulaic Hollywood love stories and the unrelenting and anxiety-provoking cultural message that you're not thin enough or pretty enough to be lovable, pop in *Shrek* and feel assured that no one, but no one, can rain on your parade.

MONSTER (2003)

STARS..Charlize Theron, Christina Ricci

DIRECTOR AND WRITER...Patty Jenkins

ACADEMY AWARD...Best Actress (Charlize Theron)

. . . .

We'd all like to believe that evil exists outside of anyone we know or might know—and that monsters are born that way, live that way, and die that way, far removed from our own experiences. It's a tidy emotional package, but in real life, monsters tend to be slightly more complex than that, and they live a bit closer to home, which makes us all very, very nervous.

In this film, based on the true story of prostitute-turned-serial-killer Aileen Wuornos, Charlize Theron brings to life a troubled woman who never met a day that smiled upon her. After many years of abuse and neglect, Wuornos finally hooks up with a young woman, Selby (Christina Ricci), who sees beauty behind her sun-damaged, hardened face. Touched by the grace of love, Wuornos vows to do well by her lover and prove that she is responsible, generous, and hardworking, but with a limited palette of skills and an attitude grossly warped by her gruesome past, she takes a turn toward vicious crime to ensure that she can "take care of business." And though she meets her inevitable fate—after all, you can't just keep slaughtering male drivers along the Florida interstate indefinitely before someone notices an m.o.—this "monster" teaches us a powerful lesson about the futility of trying to disassociate ourselves from all things ugly, painful, and hard to control.

✦ REALITY CHECK ✦

Actress Charlize Theron reported hearing many a tale from people who spent time in one of killer Aileen Wuornos's favorite hangouts after Wuornos was executed. Allegedly, the serial killer's ghost haunted The Last Resort Bar in Florida and turned off lights, knocked vases onto the floor, and even threw knives.

ADAPTATION (2002)

STARS .... Nicolas Cage, Meryl Streep, Chris Cooper

DIRECTOR .... Spike Jonze

WRITER .... Charlie Kaufman, based on the book *The Orchid Thief* by Susan Orlean

ACADEMY AWARDS .... Best Supporting Actor (Chris Cooper), plus three nominations

This angst-fueled journey into the creative heart of darkness stars Nicolas Cage as Charlie and Donald Kaufman, twin brothers who are struggling, each in his own way, to adapt to the commercial demands of Hollywood and the confines of their own natures, and find success beyond the chronic anxiety that characterizes their inner world.

Charlie is a writer in crisis who is assigned to adapt a work of nonfiction called *The Orchid Thief*, for which he feels so much respect that he's too intimidated to approach the material. Charlie, who struggles to merge his need for commercial success with his literary sensibilities, wants to tell a story about flowers and the mutable heart and soul of nature, and still make his deadline with a script that is going to wow the studios execs. Donald Kaufman, on the other hand, is Charlie's creative opposite. Donald is a self-congratulatory hack without a literary bone in his body whose solution to everything in life, including Charlie's writer's block, is to throw more sex, guns, and car chases into the mix and call it a day. As these two diametrically opposed creative instincts battle it out through the story of the instinctual and enigmatic orchid hunter John LaRoche (Chris Cooper), and his journalistic Lady Chatterley, Susan Orlean (Meryl Streep), author of *The Orchid Thief*, we come to understand that good living, just like good writing, requires us to be fearless enough to adapt to a constantly evolving ecosystem if we hope to survive, while simultaneously retaining the beauty and authenticity of the source material if we hope to ever get a feature deal.

LOVE IS ALL YOU NEED

"You are what you love, not what loves you."

NICOLAS CAGE

AS DONALD KAUFMAN IN *ADAPTATION*

"Adaptation is a profound process. Means you figure out how to thrive in the world."

. . . .

"And neither the flower nor the insect will ever understand the significance of their lovemaking. I mean, how could they know that because of their little dance, the world lives? But it does. By simply doing what they're designed to do, something large and magnificent happens. In this sense, they show us how to live."

CHRIS COOPER

AS JOHN LAROCHE IN *ADAPTATION*

POLLOCK (2000)

STARS .... Ed Harris, Marcia Gay Harden, Amy Madigan, Jennifer Connelly

DIRECTOR .... Ed Harris

WRITERS .... Barbara Turner and Susan Emshwiller,
.... based on the book by Steven Naifeh and Gregory White Smith

ACADEMY AWARDS ... Best Supporting Actress (Marcia Gay Harden), plus one nomination

Once again, Oscar recognized a movie starring an alcoholic marriage as a metaphor for the decline of Western civilization, or at the very least, as a symbol of our national addiction to codependence. Jackson Pollock (Ed Harris) and Lee Krasner (Marcia Gay Harden) lead us into the heart of one of the stormiest marriages in art history. On so many levels, Lee and Jackson are an emotional monsoon waiting to happen. He's a mother-fixated abstract expressionist with an epic talent and an epic bad attitude, not to mention an epic thirst for bourbon neat. She's a classic codependent in search of a lifelong distraction from herself. And when these two fronts meet and join forces, sure enough, the wind whips up, the dark clouds gather, and pretty soon we're all running for cover in the marital maelstrom of recrimination, hurt feelings, misunderstandings, and broken vows that ensues. But every so often, from between those threatening cumulonimbus, a heavenly light manages to break through, a light of such brilliance that it manages to reshape the perspective of the whole world from that moment forward, and remind us that some rainbows are worth braving even the most threatening of weather advisories.

OOPS! DID I SAY THAT OUT LOUD?

"I'd like to thank John Bayley, who allowed us to plunder
and I'm sure misrepresent his life with Iris."

JIM BROADBENT'S ACCEPTANCE SPEECH,
BEST SUPPORTING ACTOR, 2002, FOR *IRIS*

"Shame on you, Mr. Bush, shame on you. And any time you got the pope and the Dixie
Chicks against you, your time is up."

MICHAEL MOORE'S ACCEPTANCE SPEECH,
BEST DOCUMENTARY FEATURE, 2003, FOR *BOWLING FOR COLUMBINE*

"Thank you. I don't want your pity. I want to thank first of all the music branch for
giving me so many chances to be humiliated over the years. I have nothing, I'm
absolutely astounded that I've won for this, though the picture deserves recognition."

RANDY NEWMAN'S ACCEPTANCE SPEECH,
BEST SONG, 2002, FOR "IF I DIDN'T HAVE YOU" FROM *MONSTERS INC.*

"Oh my gosh. This is too I mean, my hormones are just
too way out of control to be dealing with this."

CATHERINE ZETA-JONES'S ACCEPTANCE SPEECH,
BEST SUPPORTING ACTRESS, 2003, FOR *CHICAGO*

"What I do know though is that I've never felt this much love
and encouragement from my peers and from people I admire and from complete
strangers. And it means a great deal to me. And if it weren't for the insomnia
and the sudden panic attacks, this has been an amazing, amazing journey."

ADRIEN BRODY'S ACCEPTANCE SPEECH,
BEST ACTOR, 2003, FOR *THE PIANIST*

A BEAUTIFUL MIND (2001)

STARS .... Russell Crowe, Jennifer Connelly, Ed Harris, Christopher Plummer, Josh Lucas

DIRECTOR .... Ron Howard

WRITER .... Akiva Goldsman, based on the book by Sylvia Nasar

ACADEMY AWARDS .... Best Picture, Best Supporting Actress (Jennifer Connelly),
.... Best Director, Best Screenplay (Adapted), plus four nominations

The pugilistic Russell Crowe stars as John Forbes Nash Jr., a math prodigy on the verge of international acclaim who is suddenly crippled with schizophrenia and is driven from the brink of the Nobel Prize to the brink of insanity. John's horizon darkens even further when he discovers that the drugs he needs to control his mental illness deprive him of his unique vision into the heart of mathematics. And then, of course, the enigmatic William Parcher (Ed Harris), a shadowy covert government operative who may or may not be a figment of John's diseased but inspired imagination, adds to the maelstrom, and for John, there seems to be nowhere to run and nowhere to hide. Or is there? *A Beautiful Mind* asks a question which apparently really resonated for us in 2001, poised as we were on the verge of a storm we didn't yet recognize: Where do you seek shelter when the storm is inside yourself? John Nash's answer seems to be: by exerting whatever control we can over the destructive forces of our nature, and no matter how high the waters rise, continuing our struggle to reach a personal higher ground.

WORDS TO LIVE BY

"Perhaps it is good to have a beautiful mind, but an even greater gift
is to discover a beautiful heart."

"I have respect for beer."

"I've made the most important discovery of my life: It's only in the mysterious equation of love that any logical reasons can be found. I'm only here tonight because of you. You're the only reason I am . . . . You're all the reasons I am."

ALL QUOTES FROM RUSSELL CROWE
AS JOHN NASH IN *A BEAUTIFUL MIND*

WHAT WERE THEY THINKING?

HALLE BERRY IN MONSTER'S BALL (2001)

No, no, no, of course we're not saying that Halle Berry didn't deserve an Oscar for her painfully raw performance in *Monster's Ball*. Her ability to create a three-dimensional character who starts as a self-centered, lousy mother but eventually earns our sympathy, and her willingness to act drunk and horny and damaged to the very core all at the same time kept us glued to the screen even as we suffered having to watch a half-dressed Billy Bob Thornton in a sex scene. But Berry also deserves a special Oscar in the category of Making an Unwatchable Movie Watchable By the Sheer Force of One's Performance: She's the only reason one might actually sit through this two-hour-long ode to psychological dishonesty that is puffed up with false sentiment and peppered with phony moments designed to shock you out of your damn-this-movie-blows stupor.

It's a shame that an actress with as much going for her as Halle Berry gets offered such mediocre fare as *Monster's Ball* and a bunch of effects-laden action pics with cookie-cutter sidekick roles for pretty women. We can only hope that the famed golden statue will inspire producers and directors to give this woman some acting jobs that are truly worthy of her talents.

THE HOURS (2003)

STARS ....Nicole Kidman, Julianne Moore, Meryl Streep, Ed Harris

DIRECTOR ....Stephen Daldry

WRITER ....David Hare, based on the book by Michael Cunningham

ACADEMY AWARDS ....Best Actress (Nicole Kidman), plus eight nominations,
....including Best Picture

Never have the waters risen quite so beautifully as in *The Hours*, 2003's cinematic elegy to the intertwining currents of love and death, which reminded us all that when it comes to the tributaries and estuaries of another person, if you panic, you'll never get out of the river alive.

In 1923, Virginia Woolf (Nicole Kidman in an Oscar-quality character nose) battles her own rising tide of depression and isolation while writing *Mrs. Dalloway*, a novel about a woman battling her own rising tide of depression and isolation. In 1951, Julie Brown (Julianne Moore), a woman battling, you guessed it, a rising tide of depression and isolation, reads *Mrs. Dalloway* while struggling to bake her husband the perfect birthday cake. In 2001, Clarissa Vaughn (Meryl Streep), a woman battling the rising tide of depression and isolation of her friend Richard (Ed Harris), lives *Mrs. Dalloway* while struggling to recreate the trivial contentment of that heroine's soiree, by throwing a panacea party of her own. As these women's lives and loves weave and unweave through the last century into the present one, and on into an uncertain future, we in an uncertain, post 9/11 world understand the idea that life could be defined in a single day. *The Hours* reassures us that while today may be the first day, or the last day of our lives, so long as we are able to invest in the moment, and even throw a theme party, we can live and die happy.

GREATEST FIRST LINES IN
OSCAR MOVIE HISTORY

"Mrs. Dalloway said she'd buy the flowers herself."

NICOLE KIDMAN
AS VIRGINIA WOOLF IN *THE HOURS*

Chapter Two

OSCAR IN THE 1990s

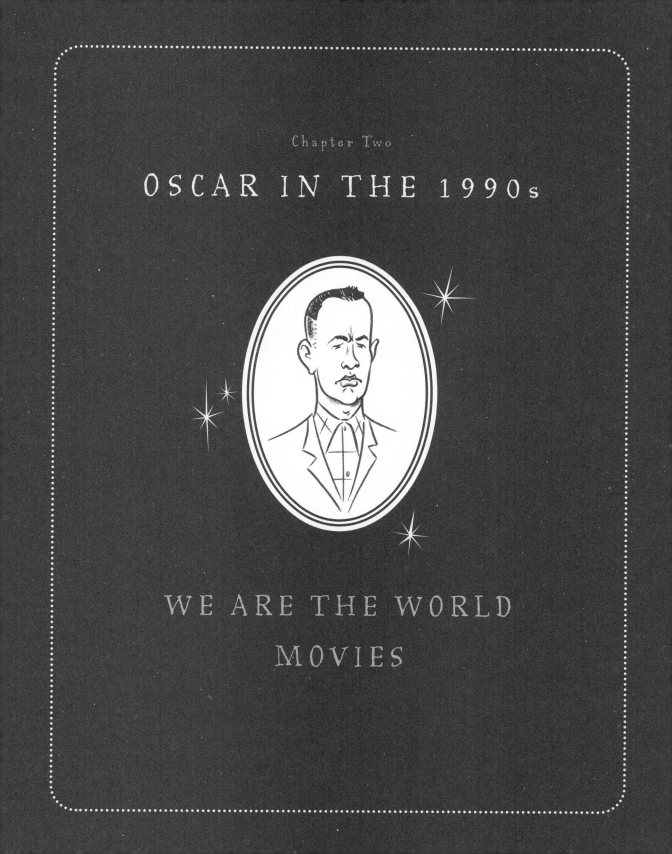

WE ARE THE WORLD
MOVIES

The Oscar movies of the '90s are dominated by sweeping sagas and bigger-than-life individuals playing out their personal epics on a grand scale. Cultures clash, social structures crumble, wars are won and lost, and ships sink. And we're talking really big ships, too. But in the midst of the global melee are heroes and heroines who, despite a few character flaws like a misspent youth, a thirst for bourbon before noon, or a tendency to snack on one's friends, are nevertheless able to transcend their own history, make amends for the injuries of the past, and do their part to heal the world, one person at a time.

So if you're feeling powerless to change your corner of the cosmos, spend a few hours with one of these We Are the World Movies, and let Oscar show you how we really can change the world, just by changing ourselves.

AMERICAN BEAUTY (1999)

STARS ....Kevin Spacey, Annette Bening, Thora Birch, Wes Bentley, Mena Suvari

DIRECTOR ....Sam Mendes

WRITER ....Alan Ball

ACADEMY AWARDS ....Best Picture, Best Director, Best Screenplay (Original),
....Best Actor, Best Cinematography, plus three nominations

· ·

There's nothing like a male midlife crisis to remind us that even the most auxiliary individuals can make all the difference in the world by cranking the dimmer switch on their inner light.

Kevin Spacey stars as Lester Burnham, a man literally dying of boredom, who finds new vitality in the last days of his life by opening his eyes to the beauty of the world and, just as importantly, the beauty inside himself. When we first meet Lester, he is stuck in a dead-end job with a daughter (Thora Birch) who can't stand him, a desperate wife (Annette Bening) who has become a stranger to him, and a body that is betraying him. On the verge of terminal middle-age spread, Lester meets his muse, a precocious cheerleader on his daughter's high school squad who rekindles his inner spark. Suddenly Lester is doing things he hasn't done in years, like blasting rock and roll while smoking a lot of killer weed in his garage, whaling on his pecs, and blackmailing his boss. While this seems, on the surface, more like dissolution than revolution, for Lester the reawakening of his desire for something, anything, sets off an internal nuclear chain reaction whose flashpoint ignites his whole world.

If you're feeling like a bit player in the big-screen adventure of your own life, and you can't imagine how your under-five could possibly make a difference in how the story ends, watch *American Beauty* and be reassured that a single light, no matter how brief, is still able to triumph over darkness.

LET THERE BE LIGHT

"It was one of those days when it's a minute away from snowing
and there's this electricity in the air, you can almost hear it.
And this bag was, like, dancing with me. Like a little kid begging me to play with it.
For fifteen minutes. And that's the day I knew there was this
entire life behind things, and . . . this incredibly benevolent force,
that wanted me to know there was no reason to be afraid, ever."

WES BENTLEY
AS RICKY FITTS IN *AMERICAN BEAUTY*

"I guess I could be pretty pissed off about what happened to me,
but it's hard to be angry when there's so much beauty in the world.
Sometimes I feel like I'm seeing it all at once, and I can't take it.
My heart swells up like a balloon that's about to burst. But then I remember to relax
and stop trying to hold on to it. And then it flows through me like rain,
and I feel nothing but gratitude for every single moment of my stupid little life.
You have no idea what I'm talking about, I'm sure. But don't worry. You will someday."

KEVIN SPACEY
AS LESTER BURNHAM IN *AMERICAN BEAUTY*

BEV'S OSCAR BASH

THE AMERICAN BEAUTY BATH

Before you hit the red carpet for your Oscar celebration this year, spend a couple of hours soaking in an American Beauty Bath, guaranteed to put the roses back in your cheeks and enhance your inner glow.

HERE'S WHAT YOU'LL NEED:

1 dozen American Beauty roses

1 cup rose water

$\frac{1}{2}$ cup baby oil

1 bathtub full of hot water

2 rose-scented candles

HERE'S HOW YOU DO IT:

When your red roses are beginning to look a little droopy, instead of throwing them out, use them to transform your pre-Oscar soak into an American Beauty Bath fit for a starlet. Add the rose water and baby oil to the bath as it's running. Then pluck the petals from the whole dozen and float them on the top of your bathwater. Next, light your rose-scented candles, turn the lights down low, and relax before your next close-up.

Bad girls in the '90s were women who insisted on expressing themselves boldly and honestly, and let their unique lights shine like a beacon, no matter what the cost of the wattage. Which was a good thing, because even in the enlightened '90s, little girls with cute little curls who could be good but chose to be horrid were hounded by law enforcement, or treated with psychotropic drugs or electroshock therapy, and sent to bed without supper.

THELMA & LOUISE (1991)

STARS ......Susan Sarandon, Geena Davis, Harvey Keitel, Brad Pitt, Michael Madsen

DIRECTOR ....Ridley Scott

WRITER ....Callie Khouri

ACADEMY AWARDS ....Best Screenplay (Original), plus five nominations

Thelma and Louise were the first and perhaps the definitive bad girls of the decade. Thelma (Geena Davis), a charming and childlike domestic ditz who has a faithless and bullying husband, and Louise (Susan Sarandon, which just about says it all) shocked us all with a buddy film about two female fugitives on the run from patriarchal injustice, who strike back at men's cruel sense of entitlement only to discover that the road they're traveling leads to a point of no return.

GIRL, INTERRUPTED (1999)

STARS ....Winona Ryder, Angelina Jolie, Whoopi Goldberg, Brittany Murphy

DIRECTOR ....James Mangold

WRITERS ....James Mangold, Lisa Loomer, and Anna Hamilton Phelan, ...based on the book by Susanna Kaysen

ACADEMY AWARDS ....Best Supporting Actress (Angelina Jolie)

Angelina Jolie's Oscar-winning wild child Lisa Rowe (yes, Rowe, and we don't think that was unintentional) was a metaphor for adolescent angst in a belly shirt, who pouted and primal-screamed her way through the wayward girls' ward and into our hearts, before being silenced forever by her own female futility. A few fistfuls of antipsychotics, combined with societal disapproval, ultimately mute Lisa's inner howl into a whimper, and render her incapable of even applying her own startling and controversial shade of nail polish. But before you go thinking that this is a cautionary tale about the cost of being an unmanageable bad girl, we'll warn you that good girls don't fare too well in this film either. The only girl who flourishes in this movie is Susanna (Winona Ryder), who learns that the bad girl inside is really just a misunderstood good girl who is hungry for the love and understanding that has been right there under her nose the whole time, just waiting for her to stop acting like such a sullen bitch and get over herself already.

UNFORGIVEN (1992)

STARS ....Clint Eastwood, Morgan Freeman, Gene Hackman, Jaimz Woolvett, Frances Fisher

DIRECTOR ....Clint Eastwood

WRITER ....David Webb Peoples

ACADEMY AWARDS ....Best Picture, Best Director, Best Supporting Actor
....(Gene Hackman), Best Film Editing, plus five nominations

· ·

In the early '90s, we were looking for a kinder, gentler sort of outlaw—the kind of fella who wanted to put all that gratuitous violence of his youth behind him and embrace the respectability that comes with speaking softly and carrying big box-office potential. In *Unforgiven*, spaghetti-Western-star-turned-'70s-vigilante-hero-turned-director Clint Eastwood presented us with a man who could eliminate the bad guys without becoming one himself . . . well, sort of.

William "Bill" Munny (Clint Eastwood) used to be a gunslinger and a whiskey swiller, but the love of a good woman turned him into a dignified, albeit hardscrabble, farmer and single father of two (his wife having been neatly dispatched by a bout with some dreaded disease before the end of the opening credits). When a young gun-for-hire (Jaimz Woolvett) shows up looking for a partner to help him track down and bring in a couple of mean fellas in black hats, Munny makes it clear that he's over all that shootin' stuff. But when he hears that their crime was a particularly heinous one against a defenseless prostitute (Frances Fisher) just tryin' to earn a living, Munny decides that it is his moral duty to give bounty hunt-

---

OSCAR FUN FACTS

Unforgiven and *Dances with Wolves* both won the Academy Award for Best Picture (in 1993 and 1990, respectively), but to find a Best Picture that was a Western before that, you'd have to go way back to 1931's *Cimarron*.

ing one last go. He ropes in another ex-gunslinger-turned-gentleman-farmer from his past (Morgan Freeman) and together the three men set out to achieve justice for all with the least amount of bloodshed they can manage.

Of course, there are complications, including the meddlings of a small-town sheriff (Gene Hackman) who so values peace, quiet, and nonviolence in his little neck of the Old West that he's willing to kick the crap out of anyone who dares to defy his authority. So, can a man with a good heart and a mature disdain for violence maintain his composure and yet achieve his goal of setting right ever-multiplying wrongs, without resorting to a good old-fashioned barroom shoot-out that will leave the masses craving one more encore? Or will he go out in a blaze of glory, doing as he's always done, solving problems by emptying his six-gun, only this time with at least a twinge of politically correct guilt?

THEM'S FIGHTIN' WORDS

"All right now, I'm comin' out. Any man I see out there, I'm gonna shoot him.
Any sumbitch takes a shot at me, I'm not only gonna kill him,
but I'm gonna kill his wife. All his friends. Burn his damn house down."

CLINT EASTWOOD

AS BILL MUNNY IN *UNFORGIVEN*

LITTLE BILL DAGGETT (GENE HACKMAN): You just shot an unarmed man!
BILL MUNNY (CLINT EASTWOOD): He should have armed himself if he's gonna
decorate his saloon with my friend.

FROM *UNFORGIVEN*

LEAVING LAS VEGAS (1995)

STARS ....Nicolas Cage, Elisabeth Shue, Julian Sands

DIRECTOR ....Mike Figgis

WRITER ....Mike Figgis, based on the novel by John O'Brien

ACADEMY AWARDS ....Best Actor (Nicolas Cage), plus three nominations

· ·

Nicolas Cage stars as Ben Sanderson, one of the most memorable underdogs of the '90s, who touched a nerve in all of us with his total and immutable hopelessness. Ben is a washed-up creative exec who turns his back on his work, his wife, his children, and himself, and leaves Los Angeles, Vegas-bound with his best friend, Jack Daniels, and a belly full of bitterness. Vowing to drink himself to death, he rolls into town, stocks up on his favorite poison at the nearest liquor store, rents a cheap room on the outskirts of town, and cracks open the first bottle. And yet, astonishingly, even in the pitch of Ben's bourbon darkness, a tiny light goes on when Sera (Elisabeth Shue) street-walks into his life. Sera, whose name can't help but evoke that old Doris Day tune about whatever will be will be, must live up to her name and learn to accept the inevitable. And while her unconditional love and concern can't save Ben's soul, perhaps the goodness she has discovered in herself can, in the end, save her own.

This bleak allegory about hope in the face of hopelessness, and conversely, hopelessness in the face of hope, reminds us that while we may not be able to change the world, or even another person, we can always change ourselves—and that, ultimately, changes everything.

REALITY CHECK

John O'Brien, who wrote the autobiography on which *Leaving Las Vegas* is based, committed suicide two weeks after the movie went into production. Rather than abandoning the project, director Mike Figgis decided to go ahead and make the film as a memorial to O'Brien.

I'D RATHER HAVE A BOTTLE
IN FRONT OF ME...

"That's nice talk, Ben—keep drinking. Between the 101-proof breath and
the occasional bits of drool, some interesting words come out."

ELISABETH SHUE

AS SERA IN *LEAVING LAS VEGAS*

"I don't know if my wife left me because of my drinking,
or if I started drinking 'cause my wife left me."

NICOLAS CAGE

AS BEN SANDERSON IN *LEAVING LAS VEGAS*

SCHINDLER'S LIST (1993)

STARS .... Liam Neeson, Ben Kingsley, Ralph Fiennes

DIRECTOR .... Steven Spielberg

WRITER .... Steven Zaillian, based on the book by Thomas Keneally

ACADEMY AWARDS .... Best Picture, Best Screenplay, Best Director,
.... plus four other awards and five other nominations

In a tabloid era where we watched a princess and a prince (of pop) knocked off their pedestals, and grungy youths from Seattle warned us that teen spirit was woefully lacking, we needed a fellow with some obvious human failings who we could nevertheless look up to in awe, someone to remind us that you don't have to be a flawless saint to make a difference. The heroic story of Oskar Schindler—a womanizing profiteer from the Second World War who ended up saving the lives of more than a thousand Jews—certainly helped cure those where-have-you-gone-Joe DiMaggio blues.

When the movie begins, Oskar Schindler is a German businessman who sees the war as a prime opportunity for engendering profits and bedding lonely gals who can appreciate a man with endless charm, not to mention black-market connections. Thanks to a few crates of chocolate, scotch, and nylons, as well as some wheelings and dealings with displaced Jewish businessmen who are stuck with plenty of capital but no power to feed their families, Oskar Schindler soon grows richer than he'd even hoped with his new business scheme. He is able to eat well, dress impeccably, and enjoy a fine evening nobbing with the big hobs, even

REALITY CHECK

Oskar Schindler saved approximately 1,200 Jews, and about 6,000 people are alive today due to his actions.

as others are struggling just to stay alive. Better yet, Schindler has a creative accountant, Itzhak Stern (Ben Kingsley), which any businessman knows is the real key to prosperity. If his new venture happens to be saving the lives of several concentration-camp-bound Jews, that isn't his intent—or at least that's what he tells himself.

It isn't until he comes face-to-face with evil incarnate (Ralph Fiennes, looking particularly pudgy and brutish) that Schindler finally begins to embrace the part of himself that values people over profits. And we are reminded that despite a seeming lack of role models, even the least likely candidates for beatification can turn out to be beacons of goodness.

ONE IS NOT THE LONELIEST NUMBER

"It's Hebrew; it's from the Talmud. It says,
'Whoever saves one life, saves the world entire.'"

BEN KINGSLEY
AS ITZHAK STERN IN *SCHINDLER'S LIST*

BRAVEHEART (1995)

STARS .... Mel Gibson, Patrick McGoohan, Peter Hanly, Sophie Marceau, Angus McFadyen

DIRECTOR .... Mel Gibson

WRITER .... Randall Wallace

ACADEMY AWARDS .... Best Picture, Best Director, Best Sound Effects Editing, Best Cinematography, Best Makeup, plus five nominations

We like stories about scrappy and impetuous young men who bravely face down a powerful and deeply oppressive force and make history by fighting on behalf of their people. And yeah, we get that when you've got thirteenth-century Scotsmen up against a British king, the conflicts are not exactly going to be confined to an exchange of witty insults in the mass media. Really, we were expecting some blood and guts from Mel Gibson's tale. But we're not quite sure why Oscar voters were so quick to embrace this gratuitously violent salute to the old adage "A man's got to do what a man's got to do." When a spiked club on a chain gets wielded overhead by a man with thick biceps as he stands over a sleeping enemy, we can pretty much guess what the results will be without the award-winning special effects of a splashy crunchy sound and a quick visual of a macerated face, for instance. (Director Gibson sighs on the DVD voiceover that this particular piece of artistry had to be cut by those squeamish Brits for their market. Wusses.) However, this gorefest influenced directors for years to come with its realistic depictions of blood spurting out of bodies as they're sliced up by swords in brutal battlefield showdowns, so we dunno, maybe we're missing something about authenticity for the sake of authenticity. Or maybe we should giggle along with the young actress who can't keep it together in the scene where she's supposed to be picking through dead bodies to find her parents. Ah, call us girlie girls, we would have preferred to read the book instead of having it spelled out in buckets of red.

SHAKESPEARE IN LOVE (1998)

STARS...................................Gwyneth Paltrow, Joseph Fiennes, Geoffrey Rush,
....Tom Wilkinson, Judi Dench

DIRECTOR...John Madden

WRITERS ....Marc Norman, Tom Stoppard

ACADEMY AWARDS ....Best Picture, Best Actress, Best Supporting Actress,
....Best Screenplay (Original),
....plus three other awards, and six nominations

Okay, we know, Joseph Fiennes looks really cute in a pair of tights with his doublet all unbraced, and Gwyneth Paltrow really knows how to fill out a ruff, and Judi Dench is well . . . Judi Dench, and where there's a Will, there's always a way. But in a year when Cate Blanchett blew the screen apart with her emotional and ethereal Elizabeth and yet was completely ignored by the Academy, giving the Oscar to *Shakespeare in Love* is a little like handing the laurel crown to *As You Like It*, and ignoring *Othello*, and really makes us wonder, what were they thinking?

"There shall be one mistress here and no master."

· ·

"I have rid England of her enemies. What do I do now?"

CATE BLANCHETT
AS ELIZABETH IN *ELIZABETH*

"I love you, Will, beyond poetry."

· ·

"I would stay asleep my whole life, if I could dream myself
into a company of players."

GWYNETH PALTROW
AS VIOLA IN *SHAKESPEARE IN LOVE*

FORREST GUMP (1994)

STARS ....Tom Hanks, Robin Wright Penn, Gary Sinise, Mykelti Williamson, Sally Field

DIRECTOR ....Robert Zemeckis

WRITER ....Eric Roth, based on the novel by Winston Groom

ACADEMY AWARDS ....Best Picture, Best Director, Best Actor, Best Screenplay (Adapted),
....plus two other awards, and seven nominations

While waiting for a bus, Forrest Gump (Tom Hanks) tells the story of his life to a complete stranger. As he recounts his tale, we begin to understand that Forrest has seen both the depths of darkest defeat and the heights of the most luminous triumphs in his life, and yet it has all been pretty much the same to him, because he is surrounded by the white light of simplicity (not to mention an IQ of 75) that guides his every step, without ever letting him see too far down the road, or even much farther than the nose on his face.

Growing up in a rural southern boardinghouse run by his mom (Sally Field), Forrest overcomes a crippling childhood illness to burst out of the braces that bind him. Guided by the beacon of his mother's unconditional love, he learns to run like the wind, and keeps on running full speed through chance encounters, missed connections, random acts of kindness, equally random acts of cruelty, a rich assortment of small miracles, and most of the major historical and cultural landmarks of the twentieth century. In fact, it turns out that Forrest has not only witnessed history but, in many cases, made history, without even meaning to. When Elvis first discovers his pelvis, Forrest is there. When Richard Nixon is looking for a hotel, Forrest points him in the direction of the Watergate. The only desire that Forrest consciously pursues is the one that perpetually eludes him—the love of his childhood sweetheart, Jenny (Robin Wright Penn), who is the yin to his yang, and who must learn from Forrest, as we all must, that the secret to staying safe in the darkness is being simple enough to never stop believing in the light.

THE REAL NITTY-GRITTY

"My name's Forrest Gump. People call me Forrest Gump."

....

"I don't know if we each have a destiny, or if we're all just floatin' around accidental-like on a breeze. But I, I think maybe it's both."

ALL QUOTES FROM TOM HANKS
AS FORREST GUMP IN *FORREST GUMP*

OSCAR FUN FACTS: ONE STEP FORWARD, TWO STEPS BACK

● Actress Sacheen Littlefeather, who is Yaqui, Apache, Pueblo, and white, didn't have a credited role in a movie until after she went onstage in 1973 to refuse Marlon Brando's Oscar on his behalf—in protest of the lack of opportunities for Native American actors. She went on to have a credited role in the cult classic *The Trial of Billy Jack*, a *Playboy* magazine spread, and a few more tiny film roles before fading into obscurity.

● Chief Dan George, who was nominated for Best Supporting Actor in 1971 for his role as the wise Old Lodge Skins in *Little Big Man*, got the role only after it was turned down by Marlon Brando.

● Native American actress Irene Bedard, who played Suzy Song in *Smoke Signals* (1998), was the model for Disney's animated and controversial Pocahontas character and provided the character's voice.

● Playing in the television series "The Red Green Show," Native American actor Graham Greene had a line of dialogue in which he grumbled that the "native guy" in *Dances with Wolves* should've won the Oscar he was nominated for. The "native guy" in *Dances with Wolves* was played by Graham Greene.

THE SILENCE OF THE LAMBS (1991)

STARS .... Jodie Foster, Anthony Hopkins, Ted Levine, Scott Glenn, Brooke Smith, Diane Baker

DIRECTOR .... Jonathan Demme

WRITER .... Ted Tally, based on the novel by Thomas Harris

ACADEMY AWARDS .... Best Picture, Best Director, Best Actress, Best Actor,
.... Best Screenplay (Adapted), plus two nominations

Okay, so the twisted psyche of a cannibalistic serial killer is a strange place to look for the inspiration to change your corner of the world. But Oscar in the '90s believed that nothing, not even sociopathy or maximum security, was stronger than the power of love.

FBI recruit Clarisse Starling (Jodie Foster) is pulled out of the Quantico nest early and forced to fly on unsteady wings, when Catherine Martin (Brooke Smith), the daughter of a prominent senator (Diane Baker), is abducted by a serial killer called Buffalo Bill (Ted Levine). Starling's laconic boss, Jack Crawford (played by the laconic Scott Glenn), an FBI vet with a ten-mile stare and cowboy courage, is willing to bet Catherine's life that his vulnerable young recruit is just the key he needs to unlock the secrets of the one man who can lead them to Buffalo Bill: Hannibal Lecter (Anthony Hopkins).

Lecter, who captured the imagination of movie audiences of the '90s like no serial killer before him, is a psychoanalyst turned serial killer, whose signature style is to julienne and sauté his victims and then enjoy them with a good chianti and a little easy-listening music.

OSCAR FUN FACTS

The Silence of the Lambs is only the third movie in history to win all five major Oscars: Best Picture, Best Director, Best Actor, Best Actress, and Best Screenplay. The others are Frank Capra's *It Happened One Night* (1934) and *One Flew Over the Cuckoo's Nest* (1975).

Lecter is, much like life, love, politics, and the NASDAQ in the '90s, alternately gentle and brutal, civilized and primitive, charming and repugnant, and there is no way of predicting which way the wind will blow.

In order to gain access to Lecter's secrets, Clarisse must learn the lesson we all have to learn when we're faced with horror and chaos: She must learn how to remain vulnerable and open to life, even in the face of evil, and to continue to look for the light, even in the heart of darkness. Clarisse Starling is an ideal '90s woman. She expects the best from herself, and she delivers. And because she is able to summon the best in herself, she is able to summon it in others also, and move even a conscienceless and cunning cannibal like Hannibal to commit a random act of kindness.

TITANIC (1997)

STARS .... Kate Winslet, Leonardo DiCaprio, Billy Zane, Kathy Bates

DIRECTOR AND WRITER .... James Cameron

ACADEMY AWARDS .... Best Picture, Best Director, plus nine other awards
.... and three nominations

Having won a ticket on the maiden voyage of the luxury cruise liner SS *Titanic* moments before it is to set sail, Jack Dawson (Leonardo DiCaprio) feels that he's, well, the king of the world (cue pullback shot as Leo balances, hood-ornament-style, on the prow of the ship). Unfortunately, Jack's elation is to be as short-lived as the comet-like ascendance of a youthful leading man who isn't quite ready for the pressures of superstardom.

Meanwhile, the *Titanic* is quite ready to take its place in the annals of history as an icon of human hubris in the industrial age, thanks to its fatally flawed design and severe shortage of lifeboats (true, the deck is far less visually cluttered, but that's not gonna matter much when that ill-placed iceberg pierces a line of holes in the ship's steel hull).

As she embarks on the *Titanic's* maiden voyage, our beloved heroine, Rose (Kate Winslet), has a heavy heart not because of any inadequacies in safety equipment or leading man gravitas, but because she is engaged to a greedy and cruel wealthy businessman (Billy Zane, in all his pompous glory) and is facing a life of meaningless consumption as an Edwardian-era trophy wife. Feeling desperate, lost, and hopeless, Rose teeters on the rail at the stern, ready to end it all, until one man enters her life and helps her to reclaim her inner fire, grace, and beauty, inspiring her to believe in tomorrow. Yes, it's out with the old, in with

REALITY CHECK

Despite its luxuriousness, the real *Titanic* cost less to make than James Cameron's movie did.

the new: the dawn of a new century, a new romance, and a new life, courtesy of that chival-rous boy, Jack. Indeed, Jack's noble nature runs so deep that he will sacrifice everything to ensure that Rose's heart will go on, even if his personal plotline has to come to a dramatic conclusion. And go on Rose does, with a full-out lust for living despite her sorrowful past.

When you feel your ship is in danger of sinking, and all the lifeboats are filling up, watch *Titanic* and be assured that you too can not only survive but flourish.

CELL MATES

Because Oscar in the '90s understood that not even maximum security bars can lock out the light of love.

THE CRYING GAME (1992)

STARS .... Forest Whitaker, Stephen Rea, Miranda Richardson, Jaye Davidson

DIRECTOR AND WRITER .... Neil Jordan

ACADEMY AWARDS .... Best Screenplay (Original), plus five nominations, ... including Best Picture

Fergus (Stephen Rea), a soldier in the IRA, is assigned to guard Jody (Forest Whitaker), a British soldier who is being held captive for the cause. Jody and Fergus talk all through the night, and by dawn, due either to Stockholm syndrome or the resilient quality of love, a fragile kinship is born.

The watercolor dawn of unlikely love soon surrenders, however, to the harsh light of afternoon, and Fergus must return home to reality. But perhaps haunted by the memory of that unusual morning spent basking in the light of compassion for the enemy, Fergus searches London's underbelly for some trace of joy, and finds it in Jody's girlfriend, Dil (Jaye Davidson), an enigmatic chanteuse singing a love-gone-wrong ballad on the wrong side of town. And of course, Fergus, being an Irishman with a pronounced sense of irony-tinged melancholia, not to mention an unquenchable thirst for stout, falls madly in love with Dil, and we learn once again that love is stronger than hate and fear, and that when you find peace in your own heart, you strike a blow for peace around the world, even in Belfast.

DEAD MAN WALKING (1995)

STARS .... Susan Sarandon, Sean Penn

DIRECTOR .... Tim Robbins

WRITER .... Tim Robbins, based on the book by Helen Prejean

ACADEMY AWARDS .... Best Actress, plus three nominations

Based on a true story, this film is about Matthew Poncelet (Sean Penn), a prisoner on death row who reaches out to Sister Helen Prejean (Susan Sarandon), a nun from his home parish in backwater Louisiana, to save him from the death chamber before it's too late. While he begins by protesting his innocence, what ultimately ensues is a story of one man's redemption through the power of a woman's pure light and love, and a reminder to all of us that it is always darkest just before the dawn.

THE USUAL SUSPECTS (1995)

STARS .... Kevin Spacey, Stephen Baldwin, Gabriel Byrne, Benicio Del Toro, ... Kevin Pollak, Chazz Palminteri, Pete Postlethwaite

DIRECTOR.. Bryan Singer

WRITER .... Christopher McQuarrie

ACADEMY AWARDS .... Best Supporting Actor (Kevin Spacey), ... Best Screenplay (Original)

When a drug heist goes haywire, resulting in a shoot-out that leaves only one survivor standing who can tell the story, five usual suspects are rounded up to get to the bottom of things, and discover who masterminded the slaughter. The lone survivor, a slow-witted and innocuous gimp called Verbal Kint (Kevin Spacey) meanders through an intricately woven recounting of events from his perspective, including frequent references to the sinister Keyser Soze, a legendary figure straight out of a children's storybook, who is so monstrous and fearsome that he makes even hardened criminals blanch. As we move closer to the heart of the matter, what we come to realize, however, is that even under the relentless gaze of the interrogator's naked bulb, the truth can be shadowed by our own preconceptions, and that an individual has the power to alter reality, just by the way he tells his story.

WE KNOW WHY THE CAGED BIRD SINGS

"I want the last face you see in this world to be the face of love,
so you look at me when they do this thing. I'll be the face of love for you."

SUSAN SARANDON
AS SISTER HELEN PREJEAN IN *DEAD MAN WALKING*

"And as they both sink beneath the waves, the frog cries out,
'Why did you sting me, Mr. Scorpion? For now we both will drown!'
Scorpion replies, 'I can't help it. It's in my nature!'"

FOREST WHITAKER
AS JODY IN *THE CRYING GAME*

"To a cop the explanation's always simple. There's no mystery to the street,
no arch criminal behind it all. If you find a body and you think
his brother did it, you're gonna find out you're right."

KEVIN SPACEY
AS VERBAL KINT IN *THE USUAL SUSPECTS*

BOYS DON'T CRY (1999)

STARS ....Hilary Swank, Chloë Sevigny, Peter Sarsgaard, Brendan Sexton, Alicia Goranson

DIRECTOR...Kimberly Peirce

WRITERS...Kimberly Peirce, Andrew Bienen

ACADEMY AWARDS ....Best Actress (Hilary Swank), plus one nomination

Based on a true story, this *Romeo and Juliet* of the trailer park chronicles the short life of Brandon Teena/Teena Brandon (Hilary Swank), who hails from Lincoln, Nebraska, and feels more like a boy than a girl, and somehow finds the courage to do something about it.

Unhappy and misunderstood, she trades her frock for a sock in her jeans and heads for her dreams, Lana (Chloë Sevigny). It seems that Brandon has found happiness at last, and he is, without question, the nicest boy in town. He's also a breath of fresh air for Lana, who is used to a town full of Joe Six-Packs who still haven't learned that the measure of a man is not the size of his exhaust pipe. Unfortunately, Brandon's white-trash utopia is violently interrupted all too soon, when he's hauled off to jail on a warrant from home, and John Law discovers what's hiding—or rather, isn't hiding—inside Brandon's jeans.

What ensues is a graphic and brutal portrayal of hometown hatred, and the violence it engenders, but also a compelling portrait of the love that can develop between people who have the courage to shine out.

WORDS TO LIVE BY

"You don't have to be sober to be able to weigh spinach."

CHLOË SEVIGNY

AS LANA IN *BOYS DON'T CRY*

CAN'T HAVE EVERYTHING, WHERE WOULD YOU PUT IT? AMAZING GRACE MOVIES

Although we all have power to affect our worlds, sometimes it's helpful to be reminded that there's also tremendous strength in accepting our situation without fighting, arguing, or giving in to the desire for dramatic scenes of revenge. In the '90s, Oscar heaped praise on a couple of lavishly filmed, meticulously painted, heart-wrenching tales about people who suffer terribly before they come to realize they've got to embrace the awesome power of acceptance.

✷ THE ENGLISH PATIENT (1996) ✷

STARS ...... Ralph Fiennes, Juliette Binoche, Willem Dafoe, Kristin Scott Thomas, ...Naveen Andrews

DIRECTOR AND WRITER............Anthony Minghella, based on the novel ....by Michael Ondaatje

ACADEMY AWARDS Best Picture, Best Supporting Actress (Juliette Binoche), ...Best Director, ...plus six other awards and three nominations

What better setting for a movie about having to accept unpleasant realities than a world war? This exquisite film, set amongst sweeping sand dunes, charmingly distressed European walls, and the devastating beauty of the Italian countryside, features a double story about people who seek love, suffer loss, and have to draw on their stores of courage to achieve grace.

It's near the end of World War II, and Hana (Juliette Binoche), a nurse for the allied army, is heartbroken because the people she loves keep being blown to bits. In desperate need of a chance to feel useful and to experience a death that isn't so sudden and personal, she leaves her company behind to spend time in an abandoned Italian monastery tending to a dying patient, Count Lazlo de Almásy (Ralph Fiennes). As his days come to an end, she will feed him plums, read to him from Herodotus, and arrange for him to feel the rain on his face one last time. And she will learn how to say good-bye—a skill that will probably come in handy given that her Sikh boyfriend (Naveen Andrews) uncovers hidden land mines and snips bomb fuses for a living.

Meanwhile, egged on by Hana and a mysterious and sinister neighbor, David Caravaggio (Willem Dafoe)—a fellow who also needs to let go of the past and accept reality—Almásy begins to recall what has led him to this painful, drawn-out death. He tells the story of Katharine Clifton (Kristin Scott Thomas), a married woman he tried to resist, but who was thrust up against him by fate, leaving him no choice but to rip her dress off and devour her sexually—very much with her approval, which makes this a steamy epic indeed. Katharine's husband, Geoffrey (Colin Firth), however, turns out not to be quite so romantic about passion unleashed by the tempest of war, and soon Almásy must learn to accept the limits of his love, his devotion, and his power to influence petty bureaucrats.

When life presents you with one grand disaster after another, let this romantic and poignant movie help you to let go of your need to micromanage your world and instead discover the exhilarating feeling that comes from acceptance.

TAKE A LITTLE PIECE OF MY HEART

"I can't work, I can't sleep. I can still taste you."

. . . .

"How can you smile, pretending as though your life hadn't capsized?"

RALPH FIENNES

AS LAZLO DE ALMÁSY IN *THE ENGLISH PATIENT*

DANCES WITH WOLVES (1990)

STARS .... Kevin Costner, Mary McDonnell, Graham Greene, Rodney A. Grant

DIRECTOR .... Kevin Costner

WRITER .... Michael Blake, based on his novel

ACADEMY AWARDS......Best Picture, Best Director, Best Screenplay (Adapted),
....plus four other awards and five nominations

In this revisionist Western in which "savages" are shown to be not so savage after all, and whites are shown to be really pushy people with extremely poor sanitary habits, director and producer Kevin Costner paints an exceptionally authentic portrait of trust betrayed and a proud people who had to reinvent themselves.

It's near the end of the Civil War, and most American Indians are unaware that those white folks trickling in from the East will quickly turn into a flood and change the face of the land and its people forever. American Union Army captain John Dunbar (Kevin Costner) finds himself assigned to a frontier outpost many days' journey from any white settlers. Unbeknownst to Dunbar, this outpost has already been abandoned by the men posted there, and the crazy commander who gave him the job offed himself without keeping a carbon copy of the orders he'd just given Dunbar. So, without the benefit of triplicated information, Dunbar sets off, not realizing that no one knows where he's going.

As time passes, it's only natural that the isolated Dunbar comes to discover, appreciate, and live in harmony with all that surrounds him, from the nearby natives who grudgingly and then openly accept his presence, to a wolf who dances with him playfully in the golden glow of twilight. Yes, everything is lush and beautiful and balanced and painstakingly recreated by a props department with umpteen technical advisers. And there's even a white love interest for our hero (Mary McDonnell as Stands with a Fist). Ultimately, however, Dunbar feels obligated to confess to the tribe's medicine man, Kicking Bird (Graham Greene), that it's only a matter of time before the arrival of stinky white people who shout "Yeehaw!" and leave unharvested buffalo carcasses scattered by the thousands across the plains. The gentle Kicking Bird, his more feisty friend Wind in His Hair (Rodney A. Grant), and the rest of the tribe have to make some hard decisions, let go of what was once theirs, and ultimately redefine what it means to be a Lakota.

When you're in the mood for a respectful celebration of the beauty of inner strength, *Dances with Wolves* provides many quiet heroes to inspire you to appreciate what was and, with dignity and courage, face an unknown future.

Chapter Three

OSCAR IN THE 1980s

DON'T WORRY,
BE . . . IN DENIAL MOVIES

Oscar in the '80s favored Don't Worry, Be . . . in Denial Movies, which presented us with heroes and heroines who overcame insurmountable odds with good old-fashioned American perseverance, talent, courage, and ingenuity. Endings were almost always happy, and the heroes and heroines got married, embraced good family values, and went to live happily ever after in a utopia made in the good old U.S.A., where there was no such thing as rising deficits, Iran-Contra, or AIDS. And because we liked our movies—and our hair—big in the '80s, many of the Best Pictures are sweeping period epics, set against historical backdrops like British colonialist India or Africa, the courts of the Austro-Hungarian Empire, or even the uncharted frontier of the dysfunctional American family. These Don't Worry, Be . . . in Denial Movies comfort us in a world that feels like it's spinning out of control. They assure us that no matter how scary things get, everything will be okay in the end, and truth, justice, and the American way will triumph over evil, just like Ronald Reagan said it would.

COAL MINER'S DAUGHTER (1980)

STARS .... Sissy Spacek, Tommy Lee Jones, Levon Helm, Beverly D'Angelo

DIRECTOR .... Michael Apted

WRITER .... Thomas Rickman, based on the autobiography by Loretta Lynn
.... with George Vecsey

ACADEMY AWARDS .... Best Actress (Sissy Spacek), plus six nominations,
.... including Best Picture

Sissy Spacek took the Oscar for Best Actress at the beginning of the '80s with her performance as the indomitable and irresistible Loretta Lynn, a coal miner's daughter (born in Butcher's Holler), who rises to country music stardom the old-fashioned way. At the urging of her husband, Doolittle (Tommy Lee Jones), who understands that the only options available in Butcher's Holler are the coal mine, moonshine, or getting on down the line, Loretta takes their show on the road, and builds a life and a music sensation, one country station at a time. Loretta is a walking, breathing, and singing symbol of small-town, southern-fried family values. And this movie is an American national anthem about an old-fashioned country girl who takes center stage in the grand ole opry of life, sings with Patsy Cline (Beverly D'Angelo), and stands by her man to boot, even though he can be a drunken no-good low-down varmint once the moonshine starts swinging back. So if your stars and stripes are looking a little limp these days, spend a couple of hours with Loretta, who cheers us on to pull ourselves up by our bootstraps and believe, for a little while longer anyway, that anything can be solved with hard work, talent, good cooking, and a bit of old-fashioned American ingenuity.

RAIN MAN (1988)

STARS .... Dustin Hoffman, Tom Cruise, Valeria Golino

DIRECTOR .... Barry Levinson

WRITERS .... Ronald Bass and Barry Morrow, based on a story by Barry Morrow

ACADEMY AWARDS .... Best Picture, Best Director, Best Actor (Dustin Hoffman),
.... Best Screenplay (Original), plus four nominations

Dustin Hoffman's Oscar-winning tour de force turned Judge Wapner and autistic savantism into media darlings, and gave Tom Cruise yet another opportunity to bask in the reflected glow with a fetching grin on his face, wearing ultra-flattering eyewear.

Tom Cruise is smooth operator Charlie Babbitt, whose wealthy father dies, leaving his fortune to someone that Charlie has never heard of before. In order to secure his share of his father's estate before his bad money-management skills (not to mention his total lack of character or his girlfriend) catch up with him, Charlie goes in search of his father's mysterious heir who is holding the purse strings. In the course of his quest, Charlie discovers a brother he never knew and learns the lesson we all must learn—there is a very thin line between being a genius and being an idiot.

For those of us living in an age of mounting deficits of one kind or another, *Rain Man* reassures us that the golden rules still hold true: Love really is all you need; friendship matters more than success; and with compassion and understanding, we can soothe the savage beast inside ourselves. And of course, there's also an ever-rotating display of Cruise's scintillating sunglasses.

BEV'S OSCAR BASH

THE MIND ERASER

If you're in the mood for a denial-ain't-just-a-river-in-Egypt marathon, courtesy of Oscar in the '80s, rent a couple of Oscar's best pictures, mix up a batch of Mind Erasers, and do what we all did in the '80s: Start drinking, and stop that stinkin' thinkin'!

HERE'S WHAT YOU'LL NEED:
1 ounce kahlua
1 ounce vodka
splash soda

HERE'S HOW YOU DO IT:
Pour kahlua and vodka into a cocktail glass over ice, top with a splash of soda, and suck it all down with a straw. Repeat as many times as necessary.

FAMILY VALUES

While many of us in the '80s were overdosing on denial and preferring to dance happily on the deck of the *Titanic* without wondering why our toes were getting wet, Oscar every now and again opened his eyes and gave us an unflinching view into the underbelly of the American family ideal. Here are a few of Oscar's favorite family-values movies, which remind us that while denial may work very well short-term, in the end, the family that can play together—and stay together—is the family that is able to do the hard work of facing difficult truths and talking things through . . . together.

ORDINARY PEOPLE (1980)

STARS ....Mary Tyler Moore, Timothy Hutton, Donald Sutherland, ...Judd Hirsch, Elizabeth McGovern

DIRECTOR ....Robert Redford

WRITERS ....Alvin Sargent, Nancy Dowd, based on the novel by Judith Guest

ACADEMY AWARDS ....Best Picture, Best Director, Best Supporting Actor ....(Timothy Hutton), Best Screenplay (Adapted), plus two nominations

In Robert Redford's Oscar-winning directorial debut, he takes an unflinching look at the dark side of the perfect American family and gives the codependent nuclear ideal a good long look at itself in the mirror, reminding us about the high cost of denial.

Beth Jarrett (Mary Tyler Moore) is a social pillar of Chicago's North Shore—proud of her husband, her home, herself, and most of all, proud of her oldest son, Buck, the apple of his mother's eye, who does everything right until the one day that he doesn't, and winds up dying young and breaking his mother's heart.

This leaves Beth with a huge hole where her sense of order and personal safety used to be, and so she promptly goes into denial about her own grief and resentment, and begins to manipulate everybody around her. One of those innocent bystanders is her son, Conrad (Timothy Hutton), who in Beth's eyes is second in every sense to his paragon of a brother; Beth even makes it clear that she holds Conrad responsible for

Buck's death. Conrad, a shy and sensitive boy, completely unlike his gregarious big-man-on-campus brother, struggles to cope with his mother's accusatory silences, his own survivor's guilt, and his father's lack of confrontation skills. In short, this entire family is drowning in the deep water of denial, and there's no life preserver in sight. When Conrad despairs and tries to take his own life, he goes into therapy and, with the help of his psychiatrist (Judd Hirsch), learns the lesson that we all have to learn when coming out of denial and back to ourselves: There is no short road to mental health, what you don't see can still hurt you, and love can't endure without honesty.

PASSIVE-AGGRESSIVE MOM MOMENTS

"Hate him! How could I hate him? Mothers don't hate their sons!
Is that what he told you? You see how you believe everything he tells you?
And you can't do the same for me, you can't!
GOD, I DON'T KNOW WHAT ANYONE WANTS FROM ME ANYMORE!"

MARY TYLER MOORE

AS BETH JARRETT IN *ORDINARY PEOPLE*

CONRAD JARRETT (TIMOTHY HUTTON): I made a 74 on a trig quiz.
BETH (MARY TYLER MOORE): Oh really? Gosh, I was awful at trig.
CONRAD: Oh really? You took trig?
BETH: No . . . wait a minute . . . ha, did I take trig? Huh . . . anyway,
I bought you two shirts. They're on your bed.

FROM *ORDINARY PEOPLE*

ON GOLDEN POND (1981)

STARS .... Henry Fonda, Katharine Hepburn, Jane Fonda,
.... Dabney Coleman, Doug McKeon

DIRECTOR .... Mark Rydell

WRITER ....Ernest Thompson, based on his play

ACADEMY AWARDS...Best Actor (Henry Fonda),
....Best Actress (Katharine Hepburn), Best Screenplay (Adapted),
....plus seven nominations, including Best Picture

Veteran movie stars Kate Hepburn and Henry Fonda were in the twilight of their careers when they made this intimate movie that captured the hearts of Oscar voters and moviegoers. With typically spunky performances, they brought to life a story that reflected our own desires to tie up loose threads, overcome any difficult feelings toward authority figures in our lives, and find some resolution before the sun sets.

It's time, once again, to open the summer cabin, and Mom—Ethel Thayer (Katharine Hepburn)—is vivacious and all atwitter about the call of the loons and the delight of wild strawberries and those tiny yellow flowers that grow by Golden Pond. Dad—Norman Thayer (Henry Fonda)—is, well, a crochety old geezer whose crusty demeanor and pessimism hide the fact that he's getting feebleminded and it's terrifying him. Their daughter, Chelsea (Jane Fonda), shows up at their summer home with new boyfriend Billy Ray (Dabney Coleman) and his son, Billy Ray Jr. (Doug McKeon), in tow, bright eyed and bushy tailed and certain that they're all going to have a positively grand time in that little cabin in the woods. But nature takes its course and old wounds become exposed as Norman finds passive-aggressive and not-so-passive-aggressive ways to needle his daughter, who can't live up to his perfectionism. Tearfully, Chelsea flees to the city, inexplicably leaving Billy Ray Jr. behind to deal with her parents' complicated dynamic for a few months. Luckily, little Billy Ray is the perfect catalyst for bringing to the surface all the family's buried issues and forcing them to face, and finally overcome, their pain, fear, and mutual disappointments. And in a few short months, Norman's contracted heart has been expanded enough so that Chelsea can bravely take a back dive into the waters of trust once again and start anew with her father in his last days.

This is the perfect movie to watch when you're facing up to your own parental issues and would like to escape to a perfect world where a few key conversations, instead of years of therapy, are all that's needed to solve knotty problems that go back decades.

TERMS OF ENDEARMENT (1983)

STARS .... Shirley MacLaine, Debra Winger, Jeff Daniels, Jack Nicholson, John Lithgow

DIRECTOR .... James L. Brooks

WRITER .... James L. Brooks, based on the novel by Larry McMurtry

ACADEMY AWARDS .... Best Picture, Best Actress (Shirley MacLaine), Best Actor (Jack Nicholson), Best Director, Best Screenplay (Adapted), plus six nominations

From the day that nervous new mother Aurora Greenway (Shirley MacLaine) pinched her peacefully sleeping baby, Emma, in her crib so as to reassure herself that Emma was still breathing, Emma (Debra Winger) had quite the maternal figure to contend with. Indeed, Mama is an Aqua Net'd control freak who will trample every boundary Emma sets. Aurora even decides not to attend her own daughter's wedding, and tells her only child, "You are not special enough to overcome a bad marriage." Ah, but as befits a movie from the era of glossing over problems, there comes a day when Mama's fierceness gives Emma unexpected comfort to light up her darkest hour, so you see, having a pushy mom isn't so bad after all. Uh huh.

Much as we embraced Aurora in the '80s, from a distance it's easier to see how very dysfunctional it was for us to be comforted by an ending that puts a bright, sunshiney spin on less-than-stellar maternal behavior. Watch this when you need to take a stand against your own mom and be glad that she's going to be a little easier to handle than Aurora is.

OSCAR'S RED CARPET: HONEY, I CAN AFFORD TO BE GENEROUS... TO A POINT

When Shirley MacLaine won the award for Best Actress in a Leading Role for *Terms of Endearment*, for which Debra Winger had also been nominated, MacLaine paused on her way to the podium to lean over and whisper to Winger, "Half of this belongs to you." The reply from Debra Winger? "I'll take half."

DEAD POETS SOCIETY (1989)

STARS .... **Robin Williams, Robert Sean Leonard, Kurtwood Smith, Ethan Hawke**

DIRECTOR .... **Peter Weir**

WRITER .... **Tom Schulman**

ACADEMY AWARDS .... **Best Screenplay (Original), plus three nominations including Best Picture**

In true '80s style, this is a coming-of-age story that relies on a reverence for the immortal courage of poets to speak the truth, and yet is at the same time a denial movie that never once dares to speak its own name.

Neil (Robert Sean Leonard), a young and "sensitive" scion of a stuffy patriarch, tortured by the inability of his father (Kurtwood Smith) to accept that he is a born "actor," and feeling hopelessly trapped inside the "closet" of his father's expectations, struggles to find his freedom before it's too late.

Neil is inspired to "come out" from under his bushel by a charismatic male "teacher." John Keating (Robin Williams) is Neil's English teacher at the prestigious Welton Boarding School, a long-heralded old-boy institution snuggled confidently in the locked jaw of New England, and which of course accepts only "boys." Neil and his "roommate" Todd Anderson (Ethan Hawke), another "shy and sensitive" student with major daddy issues, can't resist the siren's call of good father Keating, who encourages his boys to call him "Captain, my Captain" and eggs them on to "seize the day." And of course, they do, and the result is the usual bittersweet, '80s-inspired impressionistic and barely comprehensible mélange about those lazy, crazy, hazy memories of one golden same-sex semester that we will cherish forever but never under any circumstances talk about in mixed company . . . which is probably why this movie still reaches out so compellingly to the many silent weekend Whitmans in the world, now grown older, who still long to remember when poetry breathed, and there was splendor in the grass, and denial still worked at the box office.

THE KEATING FIVE

"I sound my barbaric YAWP over the rooftops of the world."

· · · · · · · · · · · · · · · · · ·

"No matter what anybody tells you, words and ideas can change the world."

· · · · · · · · · · · · · · · · · ·

"Sucking all the marrow out of life doesn't mean choking on the bone."

· · · · · · · · · · · · · · · · · ·

"We're not laughing at you—we're laughing near you."

· · · · · · · · · · · · · · · · · ·

"Carpe, carpe diem. Seize the day, boys. Make your lives extraordinary."

· · · · · · · · · · · · · · · · · ·

"I stand upon my desk to remind myself that we must constantly look
at things in a different way."

ALL QUOTES FROM ROBIN WILLIAMS

AS JOHN KEATING IN *DEAD POETS SOCIETY*

CHARIOTS OF FIRE (1981)

STARS .... **Ben Cross, Ian Charleson**

DIRECTOR .... **Hugh Hudson**

WRITER .... **Colin Welland**

ACADEMY AWARDS .... **Best Picture, Best Screenplay (Original),**
.... **plus two other awards and three nominations**

• •

Based on a true story, this rousing period tribute to the glory of victory and the heartbreak of defeat won Best Picture, and reassured all of us weary runners in the marathon of life that where there is a will, there is a way, and that the will to win is more important than the skill to win.

Eric Liddel (Ian Charleson), a devout Scottish missionary with a great set of gams, runs his races because it pleases God. This selfless notion of competition is contrasted with that of Harold (Ben Cross), the scion of a wealthy British Jewish merchant, who is running to prove that he is just as good as his Cambridge compatriots, who look somewhat askance at him because of his controversial origins. Although this movie is in some senses a discussion of what motivates champions to be all that they can be, it's also a movie that includes lots of slow-mo shots of guys running for their lives and breaking through the finish line in the nick of time, while a rousing soundtrack crescendos in the background. If you're in need of a Nike check, pop in *Chariots of Fire* and see if you're not ready to run out there and just do it.

The '80s were an era of moral crusades, and one of our favorite moral crusaders was Indiana Jones. Harrison Ford starred (back in the day before he made that scrunchy face one too many times and it froze like that) as the most lovable icon in a fedora to go up against the Nazis this side of Humphrey Bogart. In the '80s we liked our adventure heroes just like we liked our politicians: down to earth, bigger than life, without much conscience, and more often than not, wearing a funny hat. These movies encouraged us all to deny even the fundamental laws of physics, and continue to believe that we had heroes among us who were bigger than life, who would win out in the end, no matter how overwhelming the evidence to the contrary.

RAIDERS OF THE LOST ARK (1981)

STARS .... Harrison Ford, Karen Allen, Paul Freeman

DIRECTOR .... Steven Spielberg

WRITER Lawrence Kasdan, based on a story by George Lucas and Philip Kaufman

ACADEMY AWARDS .... Best Art Direction, Best Visual Effects, Best Editing, ... Best Sound, plus four nominations, including Best Picture

Dr. Henry "Indiana" Jones, a world-renowned archaeologist and all-around great guy, who is also pretty handy with a bullwhip in a pinch, is hired by his old friend and mentor to get the Ark of the Covenant back from the Nazis. The Ark of the Covenant is believed to contain the original Ten Commandments, as well as, according to Indiana, "Lightning. Fire. The power of God or something."

Together with his old flame, Marion (Karen Allen), a renowned archaeologist herself, who put the sass back into action-adventure heroines, Indiana goes up against the Nazis, and wins. Indiana Jones is a cartoon superhero for those of us who need to be reassured that a can-do spirit, and a really good bullwhip, will win out over even the most sophisticated of evil empires every time, just like it does in the comic books.

INDIANA JONES AND THE TEMPLE OF DOOM (1984)

STARS .... Harrison Ford, Kate Capshaw, Jonathan K. Quan

DIRECTOR .... Steven Spielberg

WRITERS ...... Willard Hyuck and Gloria Katz, based on a story by George Lucas

ACADEMY AWARDS .... Best Visual Effects, plus one nomination

Dr. Henry "Indiana" Jones, a world-renowned archaeologist and all-around great guy, is hired by a village elder to get three sacred stones back from an ancient terrorist cult, the loss of which has caused all of the children of the village to disappear. With Willie (Kate Capshaw), a torch-singing gangster's moll who made us misty because she wasn't Marion, and Short Round (Jonathan K. Quan), the requisite adorable eight-year-old Asian boy, as his foils, Indiana once again saves the day and returns the sacred stones to the hands of the good guys, reassuring us all that despite trickle-down economics and even Iran-Contra, God is still on our side.

INDIANA JONES AND THE LAST CRUSADE (1989)

STARS .... Harrison Ford, Sean Connery, Denholm Elliott, Alison Doody,
.... John Rhys-Davies, Julian Glover, River Phoenix

DIRECTOR .... Steven Spielberg

WRITER ...... Jeffrey Boam, based on a story by George Lucas and Menno Meyjes,
.... and on characters created by George Lucas and Philip Kaufman

ACADEMY AWARDS .... Best Sound Effects Editing, plus two nominations

Dr. Henry "Indiana" Jones, a world-renowned archaeologist and all-around great guy whose only flaw, in fact, is a phobic response to snakes, must take back the

Holy Grail from the Nazis. At his side this time, is none other than his cranky dad (apparently we weren't the only ones who missed Marion), who is targeted by the Nazis because of his knowledge of the world's sacred treasures. Together, father and son must leap the greatest chasm of all—the communication gap between them—and in a nod to the now-imminent Recovery Era, they must heal themselves from the denial of three prequels, in order to heal the world from tyranny. Watch this one when you need to delude yourself a little longer that heroes never die, they just go into syndication.

"Snakes. Why'd it be have to snakes?"

HARRISON FORD

AS INDIANA JONES IN *RAIDERS OF THE LOST ARK*

DR. RENE BELLOQ (PAUL FREEMAN): How odd that it should end this way for us after so many stimulating encounters. I almost regret it. Where shall I find a new adversary so close to my own level?
INDIANA JONES (HARRISON FORD): Try the local sewer.

FROM *RAIDERS OF THE LOST ARK*

AMADEUS (1984)

STARS ....Tom Hulce, F. Murray Abraham, Elizabeth Berridge, Jeffrey Jones

DIRECTOR ....Milos Forman

WRITER ....Peter Shaffer, based on his play

ACADEMY AWARDS ....Best Picture, Best Director, Best Actor (F. Murray Abraham),
....Best Screenplay (Adapted), plus four other awards
....and three nominations

Amadeus won Best Picture and turned a historic figure in a white wig into a rock star for the '80s.

This version of the story of Mozart's life is told through the eyes of Salieri, a mediocre court composer who is so jealous of Mozart's genius that he ruins his career and may have even taken his life. As we watch Mozart's divine inspiration grow and flourish, we watch the man himself struggling to survive in an increasingly hostile and unreceptive world, which ultimately drives him to a pauper's early grave. But of course, Mozart's pure genius endures, while Salieri winds up a mere treble note in the G clef of musical history. If you need a little reassurance that your talent will eventually win out despite overwhelming evidence to the contrary, let *Amadeus* remind you that whatever you sing with a pure and true voice will endure and overpower even the most influential of critics.

EVERYBODY'S A CRITIC

"I will speak for you, Father. I speak for all mediocrities in the world.
I am their champion. I am their patron saint."

"Displace one note and there would be diminishment,
displace one phrase and the structure would fall."

F. MURRAY ABRAHAM

AS SALIERI IN *AMADEUS*

"Your work is ingenious. It's quality work. And there are simply too many notes, that's all. Just cut a few and it will be perfect."

JEFFREY JONES

AS EMPEROR JOSEPH II IN *AMADEUS*

"Come on now, be honest! Which one of you wouldn't rather listen to his hairdresser than Hercules?"

TOM HULCE

AS MOZART IN *AMADEUS*

✦ AN AMERICAN STORM ✦

The '80s were a time when family farms were failing at record rates, and we wanted to believe that, somehow, if only they could get through one more harvest, family farmers would be able to hold on to that piece of land that had been in the family for generations. It's only natural that Academy Awards were bestowed on a few movies that promised that tough farm gals could not be stopped by snow, sleet, hail, fire, cheating husbands, financial woes, or the inevitability of change. These are inspiring movies to watch when the forces of nature and fickle human behavior threaten your own homestead, because they encourage us to bravely face hardship and keep believing in our own power.

✦ COUNTRY (1984) ✦

STARS .... Jessica Lange, Sam Shepard

DIRECTOR .... Richard Pearce

WRITER .... William D. Wittliff

ACADEMY AWARDS .... One nomination for Best Actress (Jessica Lange)

Jessica Lange, a midwestern sweetheart with big brown eyes and a honeyed voice, plays Jewell Ivey, a mom who works from dawn till dusk baling hay, cooking, and balancing accounts on her family farm, which goes back generations. When the bank sends her a sudden foreclosure notice, and her husband (Sam Shepard) starts crumbling under the pressure, Jewell finds the courage to band together with her neighbors and go down fighting rather than disappear quietly into the sunset.

PLACES IN THE HEART (1984)

STARS .... Sally Field, Danny Glover, John Malkovich

DIRECTOR AND WRITER .... Robert Benton

ACADEMY AWARDS .... Best Actress, Best Screenplay (Original),
.... plus five nominations, including Best Picture

It's the Depression, and widowed farm wife Edna Spalding (Sally Field) is faced with the burden of raising and harvesting a crop by herself, with help from her kids, a traveling handyman (Danny Glover), and a blind World War I vet who boards with her (John Malkovich). Edna sets her jaw and starts to planting, determined to prove that she's not the type to blow over in a stiff wind—or the type to alight in a gentle breeze with an easy Sister Bertrille–like smile.

OUT OF AFRICA (1985)

STARS .... Meryl Streep, Robert Redford, Klaus Maria Brandauer

DIRECTOR .... Sydney Pollack

WRITER .... Kurt Luedtke, based on the memoirs of Isak Dinesen and the book
.... *Silence Will Speak*, by Errol Trzebinski

ACADEMY AWARDS ... Best Picture, Best Screenplay (Adapted), Best Director,
.... plus four other awards and four nominations, including Best Actress

Victorian spinster Karen Dinesen (Meryl Streep) settles for a friendly marriage to a ne'er-do-well baron named Blixen (Klaus Maria Brandauer) and arranges with her new husband to use her inheritance to buy a dairy farm in Kenya. To her dismay, she discovers that he has no interest in helping her run the place—and that, unbeknownst to her, he decided to invest in a coffee plantation instead of a dairy farm as she'd wanted, even though coffee is a risky crop that won't come to harvest for years. Can this proud and independent Dane overcome wild lions, brutal heat, and a bout with a venereal disease, with only a part-time, commitment-phobic lover (Robert Redford) to help keep her chin up, without giving in to despair?

Even though Karen's farm wasn't threatened by American banks calling in loans, given our wistful attitudes about women farmers being able to hold on despite horrendous odds, we enthusiastically embraced this movie about a woman whose farm woes were as bad as any Nebraskan's.

OOPS! DID I SAY THAT OUT LOUD?

"This means so much more to me this time; I don't know why.
I think the first time I hardly felt it because it was all too new.
But I want to say 'thank you' to you. I haven't had an orthodox career.
And I've wanted more than anything to have your respect.
The first time I didn't feel it. But this time I feel it. And I can't deny
the fact that you like me . . . right now . . . you like me. Thank you."

SALLY FIELD
ACCEPTING THE ACADEMY AWARD FOR BEST ACTRESS
FOR HER ROLE IN *PLACES IN THE HEART*

GANDHI (1982)

STARS ....Ben Kingsley

DIRECTOR..Richard Attenborough

WRITER ....John Briley

ACADEMY AWARDS ....Best Picture, Best Actor, Best Director, Best Screenplay (Original),
....plus four more awards and three more nominations

Thanks to this movie, Gandhi was the man back in '82. As Martin Sheen said, "Everyone in Hollywood wanted to be just like Gandhi—thin, tan, and moral."

This epic movie presents Gandhi (Ben Kingsley) as a man with a moral backbone like a ramrod, a man who while riding a train one day is thrown from the naïveté of privilege into the dingy car of prejudice and realizes that he's got to use his newly earned law degree to help his fellow Indians. Over the course of several decades, he manages to unite Hindus and Muslims against the tyranny of the British, whose hypercivilized facade is easily destroyed when the natives of the Indian subcontinent stop bowing to them and accepting their rule. One look at the British officers whacking hundreds of quietly protesting Indian men over the head in order to bully them into submission and anyone who hadn't been paying attention in world history class suddenly understood that forcing an enemy to recognize his own debasement has the power to bring about that enemy's guilty retreat. Okay, so Gandhi's nonviolent political protests didn't change his countrymen's situation overnight and he met with the tragic end typical of a political activist. And it's true that, after his demise, the glue that held together opposing forces started to deteriorate. But the message of hope, about the triumph of human dignity over the lust for power and money, is one that inspired us as a country to . . . to . . . well, to watch this movie and be totally impressed by that Gandhi fellow, and then put on our Tracy Chapman record and nod our heads about poor people rising up.

Watching *Gandhi* made a lasting impression on at least some viewers, however, so if you haven't yet seen it, or if it's been a while since you got in touch with that can-do spirit, check it out: maybe it'll inspire you to get off the couch and find some way to make a difference.

WORDS TO LIVE BY

"Whenever I despair, I remember that the way of truth and love has always won. There may be tyrants and murderers, and for a time, they may seem invincible, but in the end, they always fail. Think of it: always."

· · · · · · · · · · · · · · · · · ·

"An eye for an eye only ends up making the whole world blind."

BEN KINGSLEY

AS GANDHI IN *GANDHI*

WAR. . .WHAT IS IT GOOD FOR?

The glamorous image of war was resurrected in the '80s with movies like *An Officer and a Gentleman* and *Top Gun*, which made being a soldier look better than being a rock star.

While Oscar still gave some sentimental nods to the movies that looked to remind us about the atrocities of war, most of which were made by Oliver Stone, there is no question that a new and powerful cinematic patriotism was being born—one that would, in one generation, come to dominate the big screen entirely, and resurrect the glory of war in the new millennium.

PLATOON (1986)

STARS ....Charlie Sheen, Tom Berenger, Willem Dafoe
....Johnny Depp, Forest Whitaker

DIRECTOR AND WRITER ....Oliver Stone

ACADEMY AWARDS ....Best Picture, Best Director, plus two other awards
....and four nominations

This is Oliver Stone's autobiographical confession about what it was like to be a grunt on the front lines in Nam, seen through the eyes of a middle-class college student who seemed a whole lot like you and me.

Private Chris Taylor (Charlie Sheen), like Stone himself, leaves hometown U.S.A. for the war-torn swamps of the Vietnam conflict to serve his country. There he is faced with a situation so far removed from normal experience that reason becomes impossible, and the dividing line between patriotism and plunder, between good and evil, is irretrievably muddied. In the combat zone of moral confusion, Chris must choose between Staff Sergeant Barnes (Tom Berenger), who represents America's pride, and Sergeant Elias Grodin (played by Willem Dafoe in his Christ-like days), who represents America's guilty conscience, and decide for himself what price he is willing to pay for his own safety and survival.

Platoon launched Oliver Stone's career as a filmmaker of the '80s who showed us the beauty in stating the obvious repeatedly, with great emotional emphasis, and more often than not, back-scored with a swelling string motif, just to make sure he drove his point home. But more importantly, *Platoon* reached out to people who were already a generation removed from Vietnam when this movie came out. To Americans more worried about the way the wind is blowing in Washington, *Platoon* grabs us by the lapels and, like a drill sergeant, shouts in our faces that we must never, ever forget, that if we don't stand by our principles and keep our eyes open to the reality of our government's decisions, things could definitely get worse.

BORN ON THE FOURTH OF JULY (1989)

STARS .... Tom Cruise, Bryan Larkin, Raymond Barry, Caroline Kava, ... Josh Evans, Kyra Sedgwick, Willem Dafoe, Tom Berenger

DIRECTOR .... Oliver Stone

WRITERS .... Oliver Stone and Ron Kovic, based on the book by Ron Kovic

ACADEMY AWARDS .... Best Director, Best Editing, plus six nominations

In this sequel to *Platoon*, Oliver Stone answers the question that was raised in his earlier movie: What will happen to Private Chris Taylor when he gets back home to Massapequa, New York? Oliver Stone found the answer in the real-life story of Ron Kovic (Tom Cruise), a young, proud, and patriotic hometown boy from, you guessed it, Massapequa, who enlists out of patriotism and sacrifices his innocence, as well as his ability to walk, on the battlefields of Vietnam, but gains a new and stronger spirit. When Ronnie returns home in a wheelchair, he must confront the pity in his mother's eyes, the disappointment in his father's, the catheter between his legs, and a pervasive disillusionment that plunges him into negative drinking patterns and a self-destructive relationship with a countercultural Christ-like figure (Willem Dafoe, who else?) who answers the question, what would have happened to Sergeant Elias once he got home to Tijuana? Finally, Ronnie finds redemption as a peace demonstrator and winds up getting thrown out of the Republican National Convention in 1972. He returns as a keynote speaker for the 1976 Democratic National Convention, telling the world, and reminding all of us, about the terrible human cost of war and the dangerous bargain we make when we deny reality.

REALITY CHECK

By the time this movie came out, Vietnam had become so much more a part of the past than the present that the film was referred to as a "period piece."

POSTCARDS FROM THE EDGE

"Free your mind—your ass will follow."
REGGIE JOHNSON
AS JUNIOR IN *PLATOON*

"I think now, looking back, we did not fight the enemy;
we fought ourselves. The enemy was in us. The war is over for me now,
but it will always be there, the rest of my days."
CHARLIE SHEEN
AS CHRIS TAYLOR IN *PLATOON*

"Sometimes I wish, I wish I'd—the first time I got hit, I was shot in the foot.
I could have laid down, I mean—who gives a fuck now if I was a hero or not?
I was paralyzed, castrated that day—why? It was all so—stupid!
I'd have my dick and my balls now, and some days, Timmy—some days
I think I'd give everything I believe in—everything I got, all my values,
just to have my body back again, just to be whole again. But I'm not whole;
I never will be, and that's—that's the way it is, isn't it?"
TOM CRUISE
AS RON KOVIC IN *BORN ON THE FOURTH OF JULY*

"There is a way out of everything, man. Just keep your pecker hard
and your powder dry and the world will turn."

. . . .

"All you got to do is make it out of here. It's all gravy,
every day the rest of your life, gravy."

KEITH DAVID
AS KING IN *PLATOON*

AN OFFICER AND A
GENTLEMAN (1982)

STARS .... Richard Gere, Debra Winger, David Keith, Robert Loggia,
.... Lisa Blount, Lisa Eilbacher, Louis Gossett Jr.

DIRECTOR .... Taylor Hackford

WRITER .... Douglas Day Stewart

ACADEMY AWARDS .... Best Song ("Up Where We Belong"),
.... Best Supporting Actor (Louis Gossett Jr.)
.... *plus four nominations*

Richard Gere stars as Zack Mayo, a motorcycle-riding, rock-and-roll-loving bad
boy with an attitude, who joins the navy not out of any apparent sense of patriotism or desire to defend truth, justice, or the American way, but because he wants
to "get jets." This was an '80s way of saying, "I want to become a macho top-gun
pilot, dress up in a really snappy-looking uniform with epaulets, slap on a pair of
extremely flattering aviator glasses, and go out there and find the best pair of
bodacious tatas in town and take her up where she belongs."

Mayo does have to face down a perpetually disapproving drill sergeant (Louis
Gossett Jr.), trade in his attitude for a little respect for authority, and get a haircut
to accomplish his dream, but in this movie, the rejection of the counterculture and
a '70s-style rebel spirit seem a small price to pay to "get jets," not to mention Debra

Winger fresh off her *Terms of Endearment* glow, with a really cute factory worker's outfit on. It is interesting to note, however, that this movie managed to do its part toward resurrecting the tarnished image of war without ever showing war at all, which is a key component in the new Don't Worry, Be . . . In Denial About War Movies. So if you're in the mood to whitewash your world, watch this movie about bad boys being reformed and good girls getting their just desserts, and if only for a few hours, get back to where you once belonged.

TOP GUN (1986)

STARS .... Tom Cruise, Kelly McGillis, Val Kilmer, Anthony Edwards

DIRECTOR .... Tony Scott

WRITERS .... Jim Cash and Jack Epps Jr., based on the article by Ehud Yonay

ACADEMY AWARDS .... Best Song ("Take My Breath Away"), ... plus three nominations

This movie was just an excuse to put Tom Cruise in a really cute pair of aviator glasses, strap him into a phallic high-propulsion object, and point him skyward, with "Property of the U.S. Air Force" stamped on his butt. Maverick (Tom Cruise), a hot-dog pilot in the Top Gun Naval Flying School, goes up against blind authority, his civilian instructor Charlie (Kelly McGillis)—who also looks really great in a pair of aviator glasses . . . for a girl—and the principles of aerodynamics to prove that he is the "top gun." In addition to the forces of gravity and the constant warnings from classmates and instructors alike to be more careful, Maverick pushes the envelope to resurrect the reputation of his fallen father, the image of the U.S. military, and a glorious vision of American grandeur that could keep us in denial for another few decades, so long as Tom Cruise promises never to go bald and ruin it all for us.

Chapter Four

OSCAR IN THE 1970s

MY HEART BELONGS
TO DADDY MOVIES

Father-issue movies dominated the Best Picture category in the '70s. Given the fact that the big issues of the decade included the Vietnam War and Watergate, it's pretty clear that we as a culture were trying to sort out in our movies how we felt about morally ambiguous father figures. In the movies of the '70s, fathers are flawed heroes who try to do the right thing, but more often than not wind up leading us into war, or wiping out rival families in a bid to retain control of the numbers racket on the Lower East Side, or just disappearing altogether. Prodigal sons and disobedient daughters proliferated at this time as well. But while the movies of this period called our fundamental assumptions about masculinity and authority into question, they also reaffirmed for all of us that come what may, our hearts really did belong to Daddy.

THE GODFATHER (1972)

STARS ....Marlon Brando, Al Pacino, James Caan, Robert Duvall, Diane Keaton,
....Talia Shire, Richard Castellano, Sterling Hayden

DIRECTOR ....Francis Ford Coppola

WRITERS ....Francis Ford Coppola, Mario Puzo, based on the novel by Mario Puzo

ACADEMY AWARDS ....Best Picture, Best Actor (Marlon Brando),
....Best Screenplay (Adapted), plus eight nominations

Ironically, one of the most compelling new father figures produced in the '70s was Don Vito Corleone, the head of the Corleone crime family, who, despite his job as an underworld mob boss, struck all of us as somebody we'd like to call Dad.

Marlon Brando stars as a metaphor for old-world family values in Coppola's sweeping family saga that created the mafia genre as we know it. Vito Corleone's famiglia is fiercely loyal, subject to rules written in stone back in an old country no one remembers anymore, and unafraid of brutality, so long as it never happens in the family room. In fact, the Corleones' values weren't all that different from your average '70s suburban family, which is perhaps why this movie, which eventually blossomed into an American triptych of father-issue films, resonated so much for '70s suburban audiences and the Academy. The Corleones always had dinner together at five, they loved their children, they never spoke against the family, they always presented a united front, and perhaps most compellingly for us at the time, the men defended their families with an old-world singularity of intent that brooked no confrontations with moral ambiguity or gender-role confusion. Within la famiglia, there was a right and a wrong, an eye for an eye, a man who goes out to work and a woman who stays home. For many of us who were awash in an ethically amorphous era where Vietnam and Watergate were hanging like the smell of burnt toast in the air and gender roles were up for grabs, the Corleones' unbreachable code of honor, and the idea that some things were still predictable, provided a sense of false comfort. So if you're pining for an old-fashioned father-ly shoulder to lean on, spend a few hours with the Corleones, and remember how much you have to overlook in exchange for that kind of questionable security.

GODFATHER KNOWS BEST

"My father is no different than any powerful man, any man with power,
like a president or senator."

AL PACINO
AS MICHAEL CORLEONE IN *THE GODFATHER*

"Do you spend time with your family? Good.
Because a man that doesn't spend time with his family can never be a real man."

MARLON BRANDO
AS DON CORLEONE IN *THE GODFATHER*

SO NICE THEY DID IT TWICE
THE GODFATHER II (1974)

STARS .... Al Pacino, Robert De Niro, Robert Duvall, Diane Keaton,
.... John Cazale, Talia Shire, Lee Strasberg, Michael Gazzo

DIRECTOR .... Francis Ford Coppola

WRITERS .... Francis Ford Coppola, Mario Puzo, based on the novel by Mario Puzo

ACADEMY AWARDS .... Best Picture, Best Director, Best Supporting Actor
(Robert DeNiro), Best Screenplay (Adapted), plus two other awards and five nominations

This prequel, made two years after *The Godfather*, takes us back to turn-of-the-century Sicily, where the Corleone family and Genco Olive Oil got their start, juxtaposed against Michael Corleone's rise to power as the new head of la famiglia. Robert De Niro stars as young Vito, who immigrates to America after his parents are murdered in a vendetta, and struggles to find a new place for himself and his family on New York's Lower East Side. The movie jumps backward and forward in time between Vito's rise to power and his son Michael's, as both of them, like their fathers before them, lose their struggle for legitimate independence, and fall prey to the sins of their fathers. So the next time you're living Dad on a loop, watch *The Godfather II* and remember that there is a very thin line between tradition and the compulsion to repeat the past, and break free to create your own, more forgiving legacies.

THE FRENCH CONNECTION (1971)

STARS ....Gene Hackman, Roy Scheider

DIRECTOR ....William Friedkin

WRITER ....Ernest Tidyman, based on the novel by Robin Moore and Edward M. Keyes

ACADEMY AWARDS ....Best Picture, Best Actor (Gene Hackman), Best Director,
....Best Screenplay (Adapted), Best Film Editing, plus three nominations

This epic crime thriller introduced Popeye Doyle (Gene Hackman), a gritty, driven antihero who spawned the popular and long-lived genre of the American cinema-verité cop film. Popeye Doyle was coarse, violent, morally ambiguous, and absolutely convinced of the virtue of his cause. In short, Popeye was a lot like we all wished our fathers would be, only with a more exciting job and a porkpie hat. *The French Connection* took Best Picture and Best Cinematography, largely because this movie features one of the most exciting car chases in Oscar film history. Popeye pursues his heroin dealers in and out of the nooks and crannies of New York's underbelly, and across the margins of proper police procedure. And while Popeye may not always get his man, he definitely satisfies the inner kid in us all, the one who wants to be reminded that while he may not be perfect, and while he may have no regard whatsoever for traffic laws, Daddy is still watching over us.

ONE FLEW OVER THE CUCKOO'S NEST (1975)

STARS .... Jack Nicholson, Louise Fletcher, Brad Dourif, William Redfield,
.... Michael Berryman, Scatman Crothers, Danny DeVito,
.... Josip Ellic, Sydney Lassick, Will Sampson, Mews Small

DIRECTOR .... Milos Forman

WRITERS .... Bo Goldman, Lawrence Hauben, based on the novel by Ken Kesey

ACADEMY AWARDS .... Best Picture, Best Director, Best Actor, Best Actress,
.... Best Screenplay (Adapted), plus four nominations

Randle P. McMurphy (Jack Nicholson), Ken Kesey's iconic countercultural hero, as played by the iconic and countercultural Jack Nicholson, created a bad boy for a new generation by standing his ground against unjust patriarchal authority—and losing.

McMurphy was the new '70s-style man's man, a bit of a rebel, a bit of a goof, who insisted above all on his right to be himself, even if it meant enduring repeated rounds of electroshock therapy and regular doses of thorazine.

McMurphy is prosecuted for fooling around with a girl who is much too young for him, and rather than serve his time in jail, he figures he'll pretend to be crazy, and get easy time at the local looney bin before returning to his rolling-stone-gathers-no-moss lifestyle. Once at the asylum, however, he is put into the care of a Joan Crawford-meets-Lena Wertmuller–inspired warden, Nurse Ratchett (Louise Fletcher), who at the behest of a perpetually disapproving and unseen father, spends the rest of the movie trying to emasculate this prodigal son. McMurphy, however—who is, after all, an iconic countercultural hero of the '70s—refuses to say uncle. He gives his metaphorical parents a real run for their money, resuscitating the inner bad boys of the whole ward, including a silent Native American named Chief Bromden (Will Sampson), whose spirit ultimately sets McMurphy free.

So if you're in a personal struggle to win your independence from the patriarchy, let R. P. McMurphy take you under his wing and teach you that sometimes you have to break a rule to make a better one, and that in order to achieve personal altitude, sometimes you have to jump—and learn how to fly on your way down.

JACK'S JUJUBEES

"Which one of you nuts has got any guts?"

. . . .

"In one week, I can put a bug so far up her ass, she don't know whether
to shit or wind her wristwatch."

. . . .

"Well, I tried, didn't I? Goddamnit, at least I did that."

ALL QUOTES FROM JACK NICHOLSON
AS RANDLE P. MCMURPHY IN *ONE FLEW OVER THE CUCKOO'S NEST*

"My pop was real big. He did like he pleased.
That's why everybody worked on him. The last time I seen my father,
he was blind and diseased from drinking.
And every time he put the bottle to his mouth, he don't suck out of it,
it sucks out of him until he shrunk so wrinkled and yellow
even the dogs didn't know him."

WILL SAMPSON
AS CHIEF BROMDEN IN *ONE FLEW OVER THE CUCKOO'S NEST*

KRAMER VS. KRAMER (1979)

STARS .... Dustin Hoffman, Meryl Streep, Jane Alexander, Justin Henry

DIRECTOR AND WRITER .... Robert Benton, based on the novel by Avery Corman

ACADEMY AWARDS .... Best Picture, Best Actor, Best Supporting Actress,
.... Best Director, Best Screenplay (Adapted), plus four nominations

During a decade when the divorce rate was doubling, women were entering the workforce in record numbers and finding meaning in their careers, while men were finally starting to ask if skipping their child's school play to endlessly schmooze the boss was really worth it. Into this zeitgeist came a painfully honest story about two parents—Ted (Dustin Hoffman) and Joanna Kramer (Meryl Streep)—who want it all, but can't figure out how to achieve it without tearing apart their hopelessly adorable, pageboy'd son Billy (Justin Henry, in a role that won him the honor of being the youngest actor nominated for an Oscar).

Meryl Streep has the thankless task of playing a mom-on-the-edge-of-a-nervous-breakdown who walks out on her little boy because her sense of self is so shaky that she doesn't feel worthy of being his mother. Dustin Hoffman, who looks ever so fabulous in his corduroy jackets and blow-dried black hair, plays Ted, a go-getter New York ad exec who has to transfer his ambitions to mastering the fine art of making French toast. While his wife is off who-knows-where, the beleaguered Ted has to keep track of PTA meetings and face down a steel-willed eight-year-old hell-bent on eating his dessert before his Salisbury steak. And yet, as the months wear on, the job Ted always thought was the be-all and end-all becomes less attractive to him than the chance to tuck precious little

Billy into bed and brush his blond bangs off his forehead. When Joanna suddenly pops back onto the scene and announces she's ready to take little Billy back, Ted is not exactly ready to revert to his former corporate-slave self and repress his paternal instincts.

What follows is a painful courtroom trial pitting Kramer vs. Kramer and featuring bottom-feeder lawyers, appalling accusations, raw emotions, a best friend (Jane Alexander) torn in two by her desire to have both sides live happily ever after, and a lesson on how not to do a custody case. *Kramer vs. Kramer* presents an honest and fair examination of everyone's point of view in a situation with no easy answers. Ultimately, it reminds us that if we truly love our children, we will find the strength to figure out a solution that doesn't deny the importance of mothers or fathers.

✦ NANCY'S MOMENTOUS MINUTIAE: ✦
BEYOND CONTRACTED SERVICES

• **Dustin Hoffman was offered a screenwriting credit for *Kramer vs. Kramer* by writer/director Robert Benton because he'd penned so many lines and scenes, based on his own experiences of divorce. Benton also asked Meryl Streep to rewrite her character's courtroom speech and give it a "woman's touch" to make it more realistic. The film won an Oscar for Best Screenplay.**

• **During the filming of *Manhattan* that same year, director and writer Woody Allen scolded Meryl Streep for not pausing in the middle of a line that he'd written with a comma. *Manhattan* was nominated for, but lost, the Oscar for Best Screenplay the following year (to *Breaking Away*).**

✦ OSCAR FUN FACTS ✦

Meryl Streep accidentally left her *Kramer vs. Kramer* golden statue on the back of a toilet at the Dorothy Chandler Pavilion. Luckily, no one walked off with it.

PAPER MOON (1973)

STARS .... Ryan O'Neal, Tatum O'Neal, Madeline Kahn

DIRECTOR .... Peter Bogdanovich

WRITER .... Alvin Sargent, based on the novel *Addie Pray* by Joe David Brown

ACADEMY AWARDS ...... Best Supporting Actress (Tatum O'Neal), plus three nominations

· ·

Despite the fact that *Paper Moon* was set in the Depression, it was very much a movie of the '70s, when a soaring divorce rate made absentee fathers commonplace, and more and more kids were struggling to win Daddy's love and attention. In this movie, there's a simple solution for the kiddies: become Dad's Mini-Me.

Nine-year-old, freckle-faced Tatum O'Neal plays a sullen tyke named Addie Loggins, whose crooked hair bow belies her shrewd ways. When con man Moses Pray (Ryan O'Neal), an old "friend" of her mother's, shows up at her mom's funeral, Addie puts two and two together and decides that while 1-800-DNA-TEST may not be available to confirm her hunch,

OSCAR'S RED CARPET: DADDY'S LITTLE GIRL

When ten-year-old Tatum O'Neal became the youngest actress to win an Academy Award for her supporting role in *Paper Moon*, she picked up her Oscar in a mini-version of Daddy Ryan O'Neal's black tux, complete with a small black bow tie and a '30s style pocket-watch chain. But Tatum never claimed she was trying to be a cuter, more compact version of Pop. Instead, she said she was inspired by that icon of '70s sexual ambiguity, Bianca Jagger, who had recently worn a black tux for a public appearance.

Whatever the real story, the pint-sized Tatum O'Neal triumphed. She not only walked away with an Oscar while Daddy went home empty-handed, she made the bolder fashion statement, too. One can only speculate as to what this did for the father-daughter dynamic at the afterparty.

there's a good chance Moses is her pappy. But Moses is aghast at the thought. He simply wants to do a good deed and drop Addie off at some nice matronly aunt's house over the state line and go on with his plan to pose as a traveling salesman and bilk widows out of their money.

Along the way, however, Addie turns out to be a better widow-bilker than Moses is and a partner in crime who's a real chip off the old block. But is Moses mature enough to truly appreciate what a prize he's got and give Addie her due?

Of course, offscreen, morphing into Dad's junior alter ego is probably not the most psychologically healthy course of action. But when you're wishing you could reconnect with Pop with no fuss, no muss, and no outrageous, attention-getting exploits, this movie makes Daddy's approval seem just around the corner.

✳ DADDY'S LITTLE BAD GIRLS ✳

Almost every Best Actress Oscar awarded in the '70s recognized an actress for playing a disobedient daughter who was acting out in a convoluted attempt to win Daddy's love. Bad girls in the '70s were a bit wounded, and when you got right down to the real nitty-gritty, they were just prodigal daughters at heart, looking for Daddy's love in all the wrong places. But bad girls in the '70s were also bold, decadent, comfortable with their own sexuality, and not afraid to make extreme fashion statements or say what they thought, which we believe was a real step forward and helped pave the way for all of us bad girls to stand up and be counted.

✳ CABARET (1972) ✳

STARS .... Liza Minnelli, Michael York, Joel Grey

DIRECTOR .... Bob Fosse

WRITERS .... Jay Presson Allen, based on the musical by Joe Masteroff,
.... based on the book *Berlin Stories* by Christopher Isherwood
.... and the play *I Am a Camera* by John Van Druten

ACADEMY AWARDS .... Best Actor (Joel Grey), Best Actress, (Liza Minnelli),

Sally Bowles is a disobedient daughter acting out her daddy issues in Nazi Berlin just before the war. Sally wears a shade of green nail polish called Divine Decadence, slams prairie oysters (a hangover remedy made with raw eggs and gin) at 10 A.M., and performs socially provocative numbers at a questionable local watering hole, accompanied by an androgynous and darkly ingratiating metaphor for the coming apocalypse. But beneath Sally's gravity-defying lashes and green-lacquered fingertips is a lost little girl in search of a dependable guy to replace her absent father's love. And of course, as most of us do, she finds her daddy substitute right in her own backyard. And then she gets pregnant with his baby and flirts briefly with a picture-perfect Hollywood ending that will make Daddy proud. But this was the morally ambiguous '70s, after all, when happy endings made us a little suspicious, and sure enough, in the end Sally decides to deny her imminent holocaust, refuses to grow up, and continues to dwell as a perennial adolescent bad girl in the fatherland. So the next time you're in the mood to teach Dad a lesson, pop in *Cabaret*, and let Liza remind you that rebelling against a disapproving father is not worth the price of personal happiness.

LIZA'S LOLLIPOPS

"I'm going to be a great film star! That is,
if booze and sex don't get me first."

....

"Mayr tells Kost's fortune every morning, and it's always the same:
'You will meet a strange man.'
Which under the circumstances is a pretty safe bet."

....

"That's me, darling. Unusual places, unusual love affairs. I am a most
strange and extraordinary person."

....

"Ten words exactly. After ten it's extra. You see, Daddy thinks of these things. If I had leprosy, there'd be a cable: 'Gee, kid, tough. Sincerely hope nose doesn't fall off. Love.'"

· ·

"My God! It's enough to drive a girl into a convent! Do they have Jewish nuns?"

ALL QUOTES FROM LIZA MINNELLI
AS SALLY BOWLES IN *CABARET*

✦ THE EXORCIST (1973) ✦

STARS .... Ellen Burstyn, Linda Blair, Jason Miller, Max von Sydow, ... Lee J. Cobb, Kitty Winn

DIRECTOR .... William Friedkin

WRITER .... William Peter Blatty, based on his novel

ACADEMY AWARDS .... Best Screenplay (Adapted), Best Sound Design, ... plus eight nominations including Best Picture

An absent father creates a vacuum and a demon moves in to take up the space that Daddy left behind in this timeless Freudian allegory for penetration anxiety. Linda Blair stars as Regan, the pubescent daughter of a glamorous movie couple who have recently separated. Regan's mom, Chris MacNeil (Ellen Burstyn), is starring in a new movie set in Georgetown, where she rents a stylish townhouse and hires an au pair (Kitty Winn) to watch her daughter while she shoots the film. Recently separated from Regan's father, Chris becomes concerned when her daughter starts exhibiting some peculiar behavior, like playing with a Ouija Board with an imaginary friend named Captain Howdy (hello!), and urinating on the carpet at parties. And then Regan starts to become bad—and by bad, we mean devil-in-a-blue-dress bad—and the only thing that Chris can do is go and find a young priest (Jason Miller) and an old priest (Max von Sydow) to replace her daughter's absent dad and drive the demons from Regan's bed.

This was tagged at the time as one of the scariest movies ever made, and even today we have to agree. Perhaps its implicit cautionary remarks still hold true: When we go looking for a father substitute to fill the void within, it's best to have a young priest and an old priest waiting in the wings, just in case.

✦ NORMA RAE (1979) ✦

STARS ....Sally Field, Beau Bridges, Ron Leibman

DIRECTOR ....Martin Ritt

WRITERS ....Harriet Frank Jr., Irving Ravetch

ACADEMY AWARDS..........................Best Actress (Sally Field), Best Song
....................("It Goes Like It Goes"), plus two nominations, including Best Picture

Norma Rae is a '70s-style bad girl on a mission who's not afraid to tell it like it is, and damn the torpedoes. Based on a true story, Norma Rae, a young single mother who works in a textile mill like generations of her family before her, takes on the establishment in order to unionize her mill. But on top of being a champion for workers' rights, and one hell of a gutsy bad girl, she's also a Daddy's girl. She is moved to action because of her beloved father's declining health and trapped in a marriage that doesn't fulfill her, because that's what her father wanted. And when she meets labor organizer Reuben Warshowsky (Ron Liebman), a man who would perhaps have made her happy, she turns him into a metaphor for an absent father, a man who comes in and shines his light on you, and transforms the world. And then he disappears just as suddenly, leaving you to deal with the consequences.

If you're feeling like you're trapped on the assembly line of your father issues, let *Norma Rae* inspire you to stand up for your rights and stop the presses.

✦

OOPS! DID I SAY THAT OUT LOUD?

"I'm up here with mixed feelings. I've been critical of the Academy . . . and for reason.
I am deeply grateful for the opportunity to be able to work. I refuse to believe
I beat Jack Lemmon, that I beat Al Pacino, that I beat Peter Sellers.
I refuse to believe that Robert Duvall lost. We are a part of an artistic family."

DUSTIN HOFFMAN
ON RECEIVING THE ACADEMY AWARD FOR BEST ACTOR
FOR HIS ROLE IN *KRAMER VS. KRAMER*

"In recent years especially, there has been a great deal of criticism about this award.
And probably, a great deal of that criticism is very justified;
I would just like to say that, whether it is justified or not, I think it is one hell
of an honor and I am thrilled, and I thank you all, very, very much."

JACK LEMMON
ON RECEIVING THE ACADEMY AWARD
FOR BEST ACTOR FOR HIS ROLE IN *SAVE THE TIGER*

"It's, uh, reassuring for me to look out at all of you and see how pretty,
and how lovely you look tonight. And so many gifted people are still making pictures
like you do with your clothes on. And contrary to what Dustin Hoffman thinks,
it is not an obscene evening, it is not garish, and it is not embarrassing."

FRANK SINATRA
ON RECEIVING THE OPPORTUNITY TO MOUTH OFF AS A PRESENTER

FIDDLER ON THE ROOF (1971)

STARS ....Topol, Norma Crane, Leonard Frey, Rosalind Harris, Paul Mann,
...........................Michele Marsh, Paul Michael Glaser, Neva Small, Raymond Lovelock

DIRECTOR ....Norman Jewison

WRITERS ....Joseph Stein, based on the play, which was adapted from
...........................stories of Sholem Aleichem by special arrangement with Arnold Perl

ACADEMY AWARDS ....Best Cinematography, Best Music, Best Sound Design,
...........................plus five nominations, including Best Picture

"TRADITIONNNNNNNN . . . TRADITION!" Papa Tevye's impassioned cry for the maintenance of the status quo resonated with a lot of parents toward the end of the turbulent '60s, and this movie was a warm and fuzzy reminder that even the most obstinate father can loosen up if he gets in touch with his deep-rooted love for his children.

It's the eve of the Russian revolution, but farmer Tevye (Topol) isn't concerned with the changes going on outside of his poor little peasant village. Tradition is his security, and he plans to have his five daughters live their lives as he has, only hopefully with a bit more money. And if they have other ideas, well, he's the man in charge.

Despite his bluster, finger-shaking, shouting, and demands that he be respected as the master of his house, underneath that gruff exterior beats the heart of a great cuddly teddy bear whose wife (Norma Crane) rules the roost and whose five daughters have him wrapped around their fingers. One by one, his girls defy his authority, each one pushing Papa's boundaries further until daughter number three's (Neva Small) marriage decision rocks the very foundations of her father's world. Heartbroken, Tevye is forced to open himself up to the reality of the changes going on around him and the limits of his control, and ultimately his love triumphs over his fear of change.

When Dad's gone past grumbly and is edging into the category of truly difficult, this movie will restore your faith in a father's ability to compromise and grow.

FATHER KNOWS BEST I

TEVYE (TOPOL): As the good book says, when a poor man eats a chicken,
one of them is sick.
MENDEL (BARRY DENNEN): Where does the book say that?
TEVYE: Well, it doesn't say that exactly,
but somewhere there is something about a chicken.
FROM *FIDDLER ON THE ROOF*

OOPS! DID I SAY THAT OUT LOUD?

"Hello. My name is Sacheen Littlefeather. I'm Apache, and I am president of the
National Native American Affirmative Image Committee. I'm representing Marlon
Brando this evening, and he has asked me to tell you, in a very long speech, which I
cannot share with you presently because of time, but I will be glad to share with the press
afterwards, that he very regretfully cannot accept this very generous award, and the
reasons for this being are the treatment of American Indians today by the film industry
. . . [audience starts getting restless] Excuse me. And on television in movie reruns and
also with the recent happenings at Wounded Knee. I beg at this time that I have not
intruded upon this evening and that we will, in the future . . . our hearts and our understanding will meet with love and generosity. Thank you on behalf of Marlon Brando."

SACHEEN LITTLEFEATHER
SORT-OF-ACCEPTING-BUT-NOT-REALLY-ACCEPTING
MARLON BRANDO'S AWARD FOR BEST ACTOR IN *THE GODFATHER*

ROCKY (1976)

STARS .... Sylvester Stallone, Talia Shire, Burt Young, Burgess Meredith

DIRECTOR .... John G. Avildsen

WRITER .... Sylvester Stallone

ACADEMY AWARDS .... Best Picture, Best Director, Best Editing, plus seven nominations

Rocky Balboa (Sylvester Stallone) is one of the most celebrated underdogs in Oscar history. Rocky was America's bicentennial hero—a down-and-outer who comes from behind and takes the title in the end, not with his wits or his wealth, but with patience, persistence, and good old-fashioned American heart and soul.

When the film begins, Rocky, a marginal prizefighter in South Philly, has very little going for him. He has no wife, no children, no future prospects, and no apparent acting skills. He lives in one room on the wrong side of town and works as a thug for the local bookie, but he isn't very good at his job. In fact, Rocky's only friend is his bull mastiff, Butkus. Yet, despite his isolation, a brush with small-town petty thievery, and a real problem with hard consonants, we can't count Rocky out. Because in his heart, Rocky knows that one day he'll show everybody what he's really made of. And sure enough, fate brings him the second chance he's been waiting for. He falls in love with Adrian (Talia Shire), the shy cashier in his favorite pet store, and trains with his perpetually disapproving father figure, Mickey (Burgess Meredith), to win back the respect he deserves. And of course, after a pep rally with all of Philly on the steps of the capitol, backed up by that rousing score, Rocky comes back from behind, and not only takes the title from Apollo Creed but wins father Mickey's approval as well. For all of us, then and now, this simple story about a neighborhood boy, and his dog, who overcomes insurmountable odds and wins the title bout for his future and his dignity, is like a pep talk for the soul. Watch this one and remember that all it takes to have the right stuff is to believe in yourself, even if Dad doesn't always agree with you.

OOPS! DID I SAY THAT OUT LOUD?

"My dear colleagues, I thank you very much for this tribute to my work.
I think that [my co-star] Jane Fonda and I have done the best work of our lives.
And I salute you, and I pay tribute to you, and I think you should be very proud that
in the last few weeks you've stood firm, and you have refused to be intimidated
by the threats of a small bunch of Zionist hoodlums, whose behavior . . .
whose behavior is an insult to the stature of Jews all over the world, and to their
great and heroic record of struggle against fascism and oppression. And I pledge to
you that I will continue to fight against anti-Semitism and fascism. Thank you."

VANESSA REDGRAVE
ON RECEIVING THE ACADEMY AWARD FOR BEST SUPPORTING ACTRESS
FOR HER ROLE IN *JULIA*

"I would like to say—personal opinion, of course—that I'm sick and tired of
people exploiting the occasion of the Academy Awards for the propagation
of their own personal political propaganda. I would like to suggest to Miss Redgrave
that her winning an Academy Award is not a pivotal moment in history,
does not require a proclamation, and a simple 'thank-you' would have sufficed."

PADDY CHAYEFSKY,
IN A RETORT A FEW MINUTES LATER

THE SUNSHINE BOYS (1975)

STARS .... Walter Matthau, George Burns, Richard Benjamin

DIRECTOR .... Herbert Ross

WRITER .... Neil Simon

ACADEMY AWARDS .... Best Supporting Actor (George Burns)

• •

In this flick, with fedora in one hand and walking stick in the other, George Burns came out of retirement to play the straight man with so much aplomb that he was able to launch a whole new comic career. And Walter Matthau proved that he had many more years of playing irascible characters before he was ready to hang up his hat.

Willie Clark (Walter Matthau) is a bit too teched after forty-seven years in show biz to wow 'em at auditions, but not willing to admit that it's time to put away the greasepaint. His nephew, Ben (Richard Benjamin), valiantly attempts to get the ornery old geezer work, with little success, until one day when the network calls offering big bucks to have his Uncle Willie and his old vaudeville partner, Al Lewis (George Burns), resurrect one of their classic comedy sketches for a variety special. Ben jumps at the opportunity and then nearly loses his mind trying to get Lewis and Clark to remain in a room for more than thirty seconds without killing each other.

When your obstinate Pop is digging in his heels, watch *The Sunshine Boys* and remember that if you can accept the boundaries of his comfort zone, life will be infinitely easier.

OSCAR FUN FACTS

Until his death at age 100, George Burns smoked ten cigars a day. He is also the oldest Oscar winner ever, having won it at age 80 for his role in *The Sunshine Boys*.

GEORGE'S GENIUS

"In what other business can a guy my age drink martinis,
smoke cigars, and sing? I think all people who retire ought to go into show business.
I've been retired all my life."

· · · · · · · · · · · · · · · · · ·

"I don't believe in dying . . . . It's been done."

GEORGE BURNS

WAR, WHAT IS IT GOOD FOR?

The '70s brought the first sobering film statements about the cost of the Vietnam War to average Americans. But right alongside these naturalistic human portraits of Vietnam soldiers who had been betrayed by their national father was a whole new breed of war movie, one that moved the drama of combat, and our issues with an absent and potentially dangerous father, into the weightless world of outer space, where things seemed a lot less threatening because there is no gravity.

COMING HOME (1978)

STARS .... Jane Fonda, Bruce Dern, Jon Voight, Penelope Milford, Robert Carradine

DIRECTOR .... Hal Ashby

WRITERS .... Robert C. Jones, Waldo Salt, and Rudy Wurlitzer; story by Nancy Dowd

ACADEMY AWARDS .. Best Actress, Best Actor (Jon Voight), Best Screenplay, ... plus five nominations, including Best Picture

Jane Fonda (who else?) stars as Sally Hyde, the wife of Captain Bob Hyde (Bruce Dern), an officer who is fighting overseas in Vietnam. To fill her time while her husband is gone, she volunteers with her friend Vi (Penelope Milford) down at the local veteran's hospital, and in this small way, tries to do for someone else what she can't for her husband. That someone else turns out to be Luke (Jon Voight), who has returned from the field of battle as a paraplegic with a passionate message to share: Don't send any more boys to Vietnam. And of course, Sally and Luke fall in love, which complicates things considerably when Sally's husband comes home from the war and doesn't share her new Luke-influenced liberal views on Vietnam.

This movie took the Vietnam War off the battlefield for perhaps the first time on the big screen, and five years after the end of the war, put the scars of Vietnam right where many of us were experiencing them, in our living rooms and our bedrooms. *Coming Home* is a great reminder for all of us that when we consider the cost of war, we ought to remember that once we make our bed, we're going to have to lie in it.

THE DEER HUNTER (1978)

STARS .... Robert De Niro, John Cazale, John Savage, Christopher Walken, ... Meryl Streep, George Dzundza

DIRECTOR .... Michael Cimino

ACADEMY AWARDS .... Best Picture, Best Director, Best Supporting Actor .... (Christopher Walken), plus two other awards and four nominations

Michael Cimino's Vietnam saga focuses on the effects of the war on small-town America. Mikey (Robert De Niro), Nicky (Christopher Walken), and Stevie (John Savage) are three blue-collar buddies growing up in a Russian-American mining town. They are the embodiment of average red-blooded immigrant American boys, and they are inseparable. They work together, play together, get married together, and take long hunting trips together, where they test their manhood the old-fashioned way, with one shot of a rifle and a whole lot of Budweiser. And as it turns out, these small-town American boys also get drafted and go fight in Vietnam together. *The Deer Hunter* shipped us overseas and gave us a glimpse of Vietnam through local eyes; then it brought us home again and let us look at our own hometowns once more, through eyes stained with the tears of Vietnam. *The Deer Hunter* makes it clear to us, then and now, that while war may slaughter innocence, it cannot kill love.

✴ APOCALYPSE NOW (1979) ✴

STARS .... Marlon Brando, Martin Sheen, Robert Duvall, Dennis Hopper, ... Laurence Fishburne

DIRECTOR .... Francis Ford Coppola

WRITERS .... John Milius and Francis Ford Coppola, ... based on the novel *Heart of Darkness*, by Joseph Conrad

ACADEMY AWARDS .... Best Sound Design, Best Cinematography, ... plus six nominations, including Best Picture

Inspired by Joseph Conrad's *Heart of Darkness*, Francis Ford Coppola's Vietnam opera has given us some of the most memorable and compelling war moments in Oscar history, as well as some of the most memorable Marlon Brando moments in cinematic history, too! The movie is narrated by a laconic and monotone Martin Sheen as Captain Ben Willard, who is commissioned to find the renegade Colonel Kurtz (Marlon Brando). Kurtz is a mythic, epic character, who has the reputation of being one of the most lethal and most talented officers in history. Bringing Kurtz back to civilization will be no easy task, as Ben finds out, and as he makes his way ever closer to Kurtz, and right reason starts to fall away, we begin to understand that what lies at the heart of darkness is fear. Well, fear, and a postapocalyptic Marlon Brando in a beret and combat fatigues, holding a really big Bowie knife. The horror.

STAR WARS (1977)

STARS .... Mark Hamill, Harrison Ford, Carrie Fisher,
.... James Earl Jones, Alec Guinness

DIRECTOR AND WRITER .... George Lucas

ACADEMY AWARDS .... Seven in technical categories including
.... Best Sound and Best Visual Effects,
.... plus four nominations, including Best Picture

Star Wars ushered in the big-budget special-effects morality that regarded war not so much as a tragedy, but as a damn good premise for a coming-of-age action-adventure series. The story is a simple one: Luke Skywalker (Mark Hamill), a young blond boy from a nice farm, whose father was supposedly killed years ago, must take up the mantle of manhood, avenge the death of his aunt and uncle, and defend his world from the Evil Empire. Along the way, Luke meets false prophets and real ones, rescues and falls in love with the snarky Princess Leia (Carrie Fisher in that hairdo), and struggles to master "the force" inside himself (which, not surprisingly, is represented as a big glowing sword that extends at will). Luke is guided in this quest by the paternalistic Obi-Wan Kenobi (Alec Guinness). The climax of his heroic journey comes when he must confront the faceless and sinister Darth Vader (James Earl Jones's voice), who teaches Luke, along with all of us, that sometimes war is just another way of saying, "Who's your daddy?"—although, of course, if you want to get to the bottom of the father issues with *Star Wars*, you've got to stay put for the next installment.

BREAKING AWAY (1979)

STARS .... Dennis Christopher, Paul Dooley, Barbara Barrie,
.... Dennis Quaid, Jackie Earle Haley, Daniel Stern

DIRECTOR .... Peter Yates

WRITER .... Steve Tesich

ACADEMY AWARDS .... Best Screenplay, plus four nominations, including Best Picture

• •

This little independent film is about an exuberant working-class teenager who shows 'em all when he wins the local bike race, making mincemeat of those snooty frat boys and winning the heart of a beautiful Indiana University co-ed—and most importantly, earning his father's approval.

Nineteen-year-old amateur bike racer Dave Stoller (Dennis Christopher) is mad about all things Italian, and his dad (Paul Dooley) cringes every time Dave rides by the old man's used-car dealership belting out arias and showing off his newly shaved legs (a speed-enhancing tip he picked up from his favorite bike-racing team—the Italians). Pops just wishes the boy would act normal and . . . and . . . well, it's not clear what he wants, because he's too busy wallowing in self-loathing to think straight. Seems that as a youth, Pops took pride in being a "cutter"—a stone cutter, that is. He helped build the local university but then thought he wasn't smart enough or rich enough or something enough to belong in the very buildings he helped create. Ever since, his passion is gone, and he's terribly jealous at the thought of his own son superceding him with a college career.

But Dave is determined to prove that a cutter's son doesn't have to hide in the shadows. With a little help from his friends (Dennis Quaid, Daniel Stern, and Jackie Earle Haley), he makes Pop realize it's time to dump the old ideas and embrace the new—including the idea that his son is a winner, not a loser.

A cathartic story, *Breaking Away* is a great one to watch if you've been pedaling uphill in the wrong gear to meet your own father's expectations.

THE STING (1973)

STARS ....Paul Newman, Robert Redford, Robert Earl Jones

DIRECTOR...George Roy Hill

WRITER ....David S. Ward

ACADEMY AWARDS ....Best Picture, Best Director, Best Screenplay (Original),
....plus four other awards and three nominations

This is a classic buddy movie that's really about a daddy-like mentor, and it promised disappointed sons and daughters everywhere that given another chance to prove himself, Dad could display a generous heart, an understanding nature, and buckets of charm.

Small-time grifter Johnny Hooker (Robert Redford) knows how to work a con, but he has a lot of maturing to do if he wants to stay ahead of the cops and everyone he owes money to. After an unexpectedly large take, Hooker decks himself out in a custom-made pin-striped brown suit that beautifully sets off his Nordic complexion and sandy blond hair. Unfortunately, such a fetching ensemble also brings Hooker to the attention of two local bad guys who want to kill him and who go so far as to murder his best friend and con partner, Luther (Robert Earl Jones). Poor Hooker desperately needs a father figure whose intelligence and cool-headedness can get him out of a tight spot while helping him to avenge his friend's death. Enter the twinkly-eyed Paul Newman as Henry.

Upon their first meeting, Hooker discovers that Henry is less the awe-inspiring mentor than their pal Luther had described: The fellow is drunk and living in a tiny room in a bordello, trying to lay low so the Feds don't nab him. But after hearing Hooker's story, Henry is willing to risk coming out of hiding to help the younger man carry off a huge con involving hundreds of men and at least one very dangerous criminal. Well, true, Henry will line his own pockets, too, and have a chance to rediscover his youth by pulling off his riskiest con ever.

As Hooker's mentor, Henry sets him up with an even classier suit and a better haircut, and begins teaching him the fine art of keeping one's cool while pulling off a double con. What's more, he even appears to be all-forgiving when Hooker is revealed to have betrayed him. In the end, however, it turns out that the young man whom Henry has taken under his paternal wing has learned his lessons well, and is able to make Papa proud of his charge.

When you're looking to be taken care of by a charming father figure who knows how to break the rules while respecting the most important virtues, *The Sting* offers a Daddy to sigh for—and an adorable son to die for.

GLITZ IN THE HOUSE

For many years, lavish musical numbers were a hallmark of the Academy Awards show broadcast. If you missed that era, or if you took a potty break, here are a few highlights—some of which were fun, over-the-top performances, and some of which must have worked better on paper than on television.

- In 1971, the show included a musical number about folks being deliriously happy to have been nominated: It was called "Thank You Very Much" and featured bit actors wearing European folk costumes to illustrate the international appeal of it all. The song was sung in English by Sally Kellerman, in Spanish by Ricardo Montalban, in French by Petula Clark, and in Italian by . . . Burt Lancaster.

- In 1952, actress Celeste Holm crooned the nominated song "Thumbelina" to her left thumb, which was wearing a skirt and had a face painted on it.

- In 1976, Elizabeth Taylor and the USC Trojan Marching Band closed the show with a rousing rendition of "America the Beautiful" in honor of America's bicentennial.

- In 1958, Mae West, wearing a big feather headdress, a fur boa, and black sparkles, vamped and rolled her eyes as Rock Hudson necked with her, and they sang the Oscar-nominated song "Baby, It's Cold Outside."

- In 1989, the show opened with Rob Lowe singing "Proud Mary" to Snow White, a musical number so bizarre it prompted demands that the Academy Awards stop already with the Vegas glitz—and inspired a lawsuit from Disney for copyright infringement of the Snow White character.

I NEVER SANG FOR MY FATHER (1970)

STARS ....Gene Hackman, Melvyn Douglas, Dorothy Stickney, Estelle Parsons

DIRECTOR ....Gilbert Cates

WRITER ....Robert Anderson, based on his play

ACADEMY AWARDS ....Best Actor (Gene Hackman), Best Supporting Actor
....(Melvyn Douglas), Best Screenplay (Adapted)

Here's a movie that captures the reality of a generation of baby-boomer men, for whom Dad was a stock figure of distant disapproval who only spoke up when his son's lack of perfection pushed his buttons.

Gene Garrison (Gene Hackman) is eager for Pop's approval yet resenting like hell that he wants it, frustrated that Dad's become a burdensome old goat, and terrified that this fate might befall him too. Frankly, Gene's got to be rapidly wearing out the surface of his molars with all the teeth-grinding emotional repression going on. Meanwhile, Gene's self-centered Pop (Melvyn Douglas) is blissfully unaware of his son's agonizing, and far more concerned with having his 6-to-1 martini garnished with a proper lemon-peel twist than with his son's need for connection and acceptance.

It doesn't help matters that Gene can't bring himself to tell Dad that he's planning a move across the country to start a new life with his girlfriend and her kids. Though he can't admit it, Dad—once the man of the hour, the mayor of his town, and a businessman overseeing 2,000 employees—wouldn't be able to bear a life without his son to kick around and inflict guilt on. Every time Gene tries to broach a difficult subject, Dad starts in again with some Dickensian story about his childhood, and Gene's feelings of shame and inadequacy crescendo, keeping him frozen in fear of confrontation. Unfortunately, Gene needs several scenes of passive-aggressive abuse scored by an annoyingly overwrought minor-key harpsichord score before he can explode into a showdown that finally reveals Dad's human side. Alas, with years of armor built up around him, the old turtle sticks his head back in his shell, leaving his son to an unresolved ending.

Looking for a chance to work through some of your own complicated feelings about that cipher you call Dad? *I Never Sang for My Father* may not offer a tidy sitcom wrap-up, but it has the honesty to admit that sometimes resolution can take many years and much heartache to achieve—and that you may have to do it without Dad's help.

PASSIVE-AGGRESSIVE DAD MOMENTS

TOM GARRISON (MELVYN DOUGLAS): You know, Gene, I don't mean to criticize, but it seems to me you're mumbling a great deal. I have great difficulty understanding you.
GENE GARRISON (GENE HACKMAN): I think you need a hearing aid, Dad.
TOM GARRISON: Oh, I can hear perfectly well if only people would enunciate.
FROM *I NEVER SANG FOR MY FATHER*

ALL THE PRESIDENT'S MEN (1976)

STARS .... Dustin Hoffman, Robert Redford, Jason Robards, Jack Warden,
.... Hal Holbrook, Martin Balsam

DIRECTOR .... Alan J. Pakula

WRITER .... William Goldman, based on the book by Carl Bernstein and Bob Woodward

ACADEMY AWARDS .... Best Supporting Actor (Jason Robards), Best Screenplay (Adapted),
.... plus two other awards and four nominations

Two years after President Nixon resigned in disgrace rather than face impeachment proceedings, this biopic of the *Washington Post* reporters who brought him down by their pave-
ment-pounding reporting reassured us that there were still father figures of authority out
there who could be firm and a little scary, but nevertheless fair, honest, and willing to trust
and guide their underlings.

Newbie reporter Bob Woodward (Robert Redford) is hungry for a story he can dig his
pearly whites into, and when the Democratic National Committee's headquarters at the
Watergate Hotel are broken into by five burglars in suits carrying hundreds of dollars in
sequenced bills, he sees his ticket to the front page. A stickler for the facts but a tad weak on
writing engagingly and clearly, he hooks up with veteran journalist Carl Bernstein (Dustin
Hoffman), and together they convince their bosses to let them have a crack at the story. The
editor of the paper, Ben Bradlee (Jason Robards), is a paternal figure who encourages the
boys to do their best with comments such as "Be careful how you write it," "Get some
harder information next time," and, "Fuck it, let's stand by the boys."

"Woodstein" is also guided by a shadowy figure nicknamed Deep Throat (Hal
Holbrook), who meets Woodward in dark parking garages to let him know when he's on the
right track, scolding him when he messes up, and offering the rare piece of mysterious advice
like "Follow the money." Ultimately, our hardworking and honest boys make their daddies
proud and remind us all that when dear old dad disappoints, we can still find father substi-
tutes who satisfy our need for kindly guidance and approval.

FATHER KNOWS BEST II

"You know the results of the latest Gallup Poll? Half the country never even heard of the word Watergate. Nobody gives a shit. You guys are probably pretty tired, right? Well, you should be. Go on home, get a nice hot bath. Rest up . . . fifteen minutes. Then get your asses back in gear. We're under a lot of pressure, you know, and you put us there. Nothing's riding on this except the, uh, First Amendment to the Constitution, freedom of the press, and maybe the future of the country. Not that any of that matters, but if you guys fuck up again, I'm going to get mad. Goodnight."

· · · · · · · · · · · · · · · · ·

"Now hold it, hold it. We're about to accuse Haldeman,
who only happens to be the second most important man in this country,
of conducting a criminal conspiracy from inside the White House.
It would be nice if we were right."

JASON ROBARDS

AS BEN BRADLEE IN *ALL THE PRESIDENT'S MEN*

"Forget the myths the media's created about the White House.
The truth is, these are not very bright guys, and things got out of hand."

· · · · · · · · · · · · · · · · ·

"Follow the money."

HAL HOLBROOK

AS DEEP THROAT IN *ALL THE PRESIDENT'S MEN*

THE PAPER CHASE (1973)

STARS ....Timothy Bottoms, John Houseman, Lindsey Wagner

DIRECTOR AND WRITER ....James Bridges, based on the novel by John J. Osborn Jr.

ACADEMY AWARDS ....Best Supporting Actor (John Houseman), plus two nominations

· ·

For all those shaggy-haired '70s dudes who couldn't win Dad's acceptance no matter how hard they tried, *The Paper Chase* offered the promise of reaching that elusive goal—even if Dad's approval didn't go much beyond a grunt in passing.

At Harvard Law School, the notorious Professor Kingsfield (John Houseman) is a stern, bow-tied, stiff-backed father figure who baffles, frustrates, and totally intimidates his substitute children: the first-year law students who are desperate to pass his contracts law class. One pseudo-son is Mr. Hart (Timothy Bottoms), or rather, Mister HAHHRRRT. Kingsfield, it seems, can make a wide-eyed freshman quiver with anxiety, just by calling the poor slob's name out in that resonant Boston Brahmin accent of his. Butterflies aside, Hart is absolutely determined to not only ace the class but make Kingsfield notice him without having to consult the seating chart. Maybe Kingsfield will even pat him on the head by offering Hart the glorious honor of doing gruntwork on some legal paper the professor has to generate. Meanwhile, Kingsfield's daughter, Susan (Lindsey Wagner), has started an affair with Hart, and keeps urging her boyfriend to give up his need for order and structure and go with that '70s live-in-the-moment flow. Frankly, she wishes he'd create some better pillow talk than blathering on about what really makes her dad tick. Then again, if she doesn't want the shadow of her father cast over them, she probably shouldn't be screwing Hart in Daddy's bed. Yup, she's got Daddy issues, too.

This is a great one to watch when you want a good laugh at your own neurotic need to obsess over the details of how to get that tiny corner of Daddy's mouth to move upward infinitesimally in a barely discernable gesture of approbation.

FATHER KNOWS BEST III

"LOUDLY, Mister Haaaahhrrrt.
FILL this room with your INTELLIGENCE."

. . . .

"At times, you may feel that you have found the correct answer.
I assure you, this is a TOTAL DELUSION on your part."

. . . .

"You come in here with a skullful of MUSH,
and you LEAVE thinking like a LAWYER."

ALL QUOTES FROM JOHN HOUSEMAN
AS PROFESSOR KINGSFIELD IN *THE PAPER CHASE*

Chapter Five

OSCAR IN THE 1960s

GIVE PEACE A CHANCE
MOVIES

The '60s were a time of great social upheaval, and everybody from Akron to Ashtabula was pretty much feeling the heat of the civil rights movement, the women's movement, the assassination of President Kennedy, and the Vietnam War. It's no wonder then that audiences looked to the movies for escape from the stress of living through such a remarkable decade. The Give Peace a Chance Movies in this chapter offered America a variety of peaceful alternatives to their stressful lives, from period dramas about better times to fiercely personal pleas to give peace a chance, providing a traumatized America a few hours of welcome relief and a little good, not-so-clean fun.

THE SOUND OF MUSIC (1965)

STARS ....Julie Andrews, Christopher Plummer

DIRECTOR ....Robert Wise

WRITERS ....Ernest Lehman,
............................based on the book *The Trapp Family Singers* by Maria Von Trapp

ACADEMY AWARDS ....Best Picture, Best Director,
....plus three other awards and five nominations

· ·

The Vietnam War was escalating; civil rights movement activists and leaders were being hosed down, arrested, and even murdered; and we all just wanted to don a pinafore, spin around, and sing to the lovely Alps about how wonderful life was. Okay, maybe *The Sound of Music*'s success in 1965 does make you think a whole lot of folks desperately needed to deny reality. But if you can get past its sugary exterior and too-cute band of rosy-cheeked youngsters, you might be able to buy into the idea that music can unite us even as it expresses our individuality and eases our fears.

Maria (Julie Andrews) is a novice nun who doesn't seem to fit in to the convent community, and is asked by her mother superior (Peggy Wood) to work as a nanny for a widowed baron (Christopher Plummer) who needs a woman's touch in his life. After all, the baron has his kids marching around to the sound of a whistle and lining up like small soldiers for roll call. They put on a united front for Papa, but frankly, they all just want a mom to hold them during thunderstorms. Maria brings the force of the feminine to the house, and gently nudges the children to give up their antagonism toward her. By teaching them about the joys of singing together in harmony, she alleviates their need to define themselves through obstinate and bratty behavior, and eventually unites the whole family through song—which turns out to be their ticket out of oppression and fear, not to mention their ticket out of a country facing war and upheaval.

Perhaps songs about whiskers on kittens or lonely goatherds—oha layhee oha layhee oha layhee ho—don't make you feel warm and fuzzy. But if you're a sucker for sentimentality, you might find *The Sound of Music* a cozy reminder that a bit of song can envelope you in a whole lot of love.

LAWRENCE OF ARABIA (1962)

STARS .... Peter O'Toole, Alec Guinness, Anthony Quinn,
.... Jack Hawkins, Omar Sharif, José Ferrer,
.... Anthony Quayle, Claude Rains, Arthur Kennedy, Donald Wolfit

DIRECTOR .... David Lean

WRITERS .... Robert Bolt, Michael Wilson, based on the writings of T. E. Lawrence

ACADEMY AWARDS .... Best Picture, Best Director,
.... plus five other awards and three nominations

Lawrence of Arabia, David Lean's desert epic, is less a movie than an experience. The need for peace and cooperation with one's fellow man is visually evident in the sweeping desert that turns men into barely discernible specks, and where the greatest triumphs and tragedies of men are as small and mutable as wind sketches in the sand. At the center of this ponderous landscape is Lawrence himself (Peter O'Toole). T. E. Lawrence was a real figure in history, an eccentric British soldier who was bored with his job as a cartographer and crossed the desert on the back of a camel to unite the warring tribes of Saudi Arabia and lead them to victory against the Turks. O'Toole's Lawrence is lean, angular, soft-spoken, and sensitive. And of course, he's got those amazing blue eyes that seem to pierce through the desert heat and jump right into your lap. But what is perhaps most resonant, beyond the exotic visual grandeur, is the idea that a commander could be powerful because he was merciful; that he could be cruel to be kind, and victorious in battle, because he loved peace.

DIAMONDS FROM THE DESERT

Club Secretary (Jack Gwillim): I say, Lawrence. You are a clown!

T. E. Lawrence (Peter O'Toole): We can't all be lion tamers.

· · · · · · · · · · · · · · · · ·

General Allenby (Jack Hawkins): I'm promoting you, Major.

T. E. Lawrence (Peter O'Toole): I don't think that's a very good idea.

· · · · · · · · · · · · · · · · ·

General Murray (Donald Wolfit): I can't make out whether you're a bloody madman or
just half-witted.

T. E. Lawrence (Peter O'Toole): I have the same problem, sir.

· · · · · · · · · · · · · · · · ·

Jackson Bentley (Arthur Kennedy): What attracts you personally to the desert?

T. E. Lawrence (Peter O'Toole): It's clean.

· · · · · · · · · · · · · · · · ·

"Nothing is written."

PETER O'TOOLE

AS LAWRENCE

ALL QUOTES FROM *LAWRENCE OF ARABIA*

A MAN FOR ALL SEASONS (1966)

STARS ....Paul Scofield, Wendy Hiller, Leo McKern, Robert Shaw,
....Orson Welles, Susannah York, Nigel Davenport, John Hurt

DIRECTOR ....Fred Zinnemann

WRITER ....Robert Bolt, based on his play

ACADEMY AWARDS ....Best Picture, Best Director, Best Actor,
....Best Screenplay (Adapted), plus two other awards and two nominations

This big-screen biography of Sir Thomas More (Paul Scofield), who stood up against a corrupt government and paid for it with his life, touched a chord for audiences in the '60s, who understood a thing or two about government corruption and giving your life for a cause.

Scofield's More is a mild and reasonable middle-aged clergyman with a loving and faithful wife, Alice (Wendy Hiller), and a daughter, Margaret (Susannah York), who adores him. Thomas's life should have run a tranquil, predictable, and privileged course, but everything changes when his friend King Henry VIII (Robert Shaw), who has appointed him chancellor, decides that he wants to get a divorce and demands Thomas's approval. More refuses to sanction Henry's proposed split from the Catholic church, which would permit Henry to divorce his wife and marry someone who can produce an heir to the throne. History tells us who won and who lost that battle. The historic saga, however, is just a jacket to dress up what this movie is really about: a patient, noble, peaceful resister, who stands up to city hall without ever raising his hand in anger, and whose righteous silence spoke louder than words.

THOMAS'S TIMELESS TIDBITS

"I think that when statesmen forsake their own private conscience for the sake of their public duties, they lead their country by a short route to chaos."

PAUL SCOFIELD

AS SIR THOMAS MORE IN *A MAN FOR ALL SEASONS*

MARY POPPINS (1964)

STARS ....Julie Andrews, Dick Van Dyke,
....................................David Tomlinson, Glynis Johns, Karen Dotrice, Matthew Garber

DIRECTOR ....Robert Stevenson

WRITERS ....Bill Walsh, Don da Gradi,
....based on the Mary Poppins books by P. L. Travers

ACADEMY AWARDS ....Best Actress,
....................................plus four other awards and eight nominations, including Best Picture

We know you're thinking that this is one of those saccharine Disney live-action movies from the post-animation, pre-Eisner, pre-Pixar years that you vaguely remember from childhood. But of course, when you were in your spoonful-of-sugar years, you probably didn't catch *Mary Poppins'* delightfully subversive messages about upending capitalist priorities and rejecting a fear-based narrow-minded pursuit of money and financial security in favor of reconnecting with those you love. In this flick, five-foot-tall hat stands fit into carpet bags, children can clean their playrooms with a snap of a finger, and anyone can jump into the landscape of a sidewalk chalk drawing and spend the afternoon riding a carousel horse through the countryside.

It is 1910, and Mr. Banks (David Tomlinson) is the proud papa of an Edwardian family that he thinks hangs on his every word—except that in reality, his wife (Glynis Johns) is too busy running off to suffragette meetings to pay him or the kids much mind, and his children, Jane (Karen Dotrice) and Michael (Matthew Garber), keep ditching their caregivers

WARNING LABEL

Should a potential nanny bearing no references come floating down on a zephyr to your front door, we suggest you make a quick call to the agency before hiring . . . or at least install a nanny cam in the playroom.

in the park. Enter the ultimate nanny, Mary Poppins (Julie Andrews), drifting down from the heavens with her umbrella and carpet bag in hand, ready to slide up banisters, encourage the children to break the rules of physics, and teach Mr. and Mrs. Banks to neglect their outside obligations and go fly a kite in the park with Jane and Michael. Egging on the redoubtable Mary Poppins is a chimney sweep/one-man band/chalk artist/kite salesman named Bert (Dick Van Dyke), who sings, tap-dances across rooftops, and merrily laughs his days away, unfettered by the 9 to 5 world or preconceived notions about gravity and dimension.

Beleaguered by the daily grind and in need of a magical reminder that your connections with others, not money, are what make the world go round? Play hooky, pop in this movie, and have a jolly holiday with Mary.

THE WORLD ACCORDING TO
MARY POPPINS

"First of all, I'd like to make one thing quite clear . . . I never explain anything."

. . . .

"In every job that must be done, there is an element of fun.
You find the fun and snap! The job's a game."

. . . .

"Of course, you can say it backwards, which is dociousaliexpilisticfragicalirupus, but that's going a bit too far, don't you think?"

JULIE ANDREWS
AS MARY POPPINS IN *MARY POPPINS*

THE BATTLE OF THE SEXES

In this "give peace a chance" era, one of the battles that was being fought full-throttle was the war between the sexes. In the '60s, husbands and wives by the dozen duked it out onscreen, and if we take a cue from these pictures, there weren't going to be any winners until we finally put down our boxing gloves and learned to trust each other.

WHO'S AFRAID OF VIRGINIA WOOLF? (1966)

STARS .... Elizabeth Taylor, Richard Burton, Sandy Dennis, George Segal

DIRECTOR .... Mike Nichols

WRITER .... Ernest Lehman, based on the play by Edward Albee

ACADEMY AWARDS .... Best Actress (Elizabeth Taylor),
.... Best Supporting Actress (Sandy Dennis),
.... plus three other awards and eight nominations, including Best Picture

In Edward Albee's classic tale of a university professor's daughter and her 100-proof self-loathing, Elizabeth Taylor stars as the boozy and blousy Martha who manages to stagger her way through the long night of a bad marriage and into the sober dawn of redemption, with a rocks glass in her hand.

From the very first gin rickey, Martha is inexorably sipping her way toward a marital exorcism that will ultimately free her marriage from the demons of distrust, denial, and self-hatred. In the end, redemption comes in the form of a new day of trust and honesty between husband and wife, who at last are able to retire to bed, arm in arm, because they can admit that they are afraid of Virginia Woolf, especially after a fourth martini.

MARTHA, MARTHA, MARTHA!

"Martha, in my mind you're buried in cement right up to the neck.
No, up to the nose, it's much quieter."

RICHARD BURTON

AS GEORGE IN *WHO'S AFRAID OF VIRGINIA WOOLF?*

"I'm tired, I've been drinking since nine o'clock, my wife is vomiting,
there's been a lot of screaming going on around here!"

GEORGE SEGAL

AS NICK IN *WHO'S AFRAID OF VIRGINIA WOOLF?*

"You're all flops. I am the Earth Mother, and you are all flops."

ELIZABETH TAYLOR

AS MARTHA IN *WHO'S AFRAID OF VIRGINIA WOOLF?*

THE LION IN WINTER (1968)

STARS .... Katharine Hepburn, Peter O'Toole, Anthony Hopkins,
.... John Castle, Nigel Terry, Timothy Dalton, Jane Merrow

DIRECTOR .... Anthony Harvey

WRITER .... James Goldman, based on his play

ACADEMY AWARDS .... Best Actress, Best Screenplay (Adapted),
.... plus one other award and four nominations, including Best Picture

Katharine Hepburn and Peter O'Toole star as King Henry III and his queen,
Eleanor of Aquitaine, whose struggles for the succession of the crown provided
movie audiences with a big box-office metaphor for the gender power struggles
going on between men and women in the '60s. Henry, who doesn't trust his wife,
and for very good reason (she's raised two revolutions against him), makes sure she
spends her days in solitary confinement in a convent somewhere, except on holi-

days when she is invited to Henry's court. And because life can be much kinder for kings, Henry wiles away his middle age with his teenage French mistress, Princess Alais (Jane Merrow), whom he must shortly marry off to his son, John (Nigel Terry), to solidify his favorite son's sucession to the crown. But then Christmas comes, which means Queen Eleanor is arriving for a visit, and Eleanor has different ideas about who will wear the crown of England. What ensues is a battle to the death between the members of this dysfunctional family, but at its core, it's a plea for peace: peace between nations, between families, and between men and women.

ELEANOR'S EGG CREAMS

"In a world where carpenters get resurrected, everything is possible."

....

"I could peel you like a pear and God himself would call it justice!"

....

"What would you have me do? Give out? Give up? Give in?"

....

"I made Louis take me on Crusade. I dressed my women as Amazons
and we rode bare-breasted halfway to Damascus.
Louis had a seizure and I damn near died of windburn...
but the troops were dazzled."

....

"Of course he has a knife, he always has a knife, we all have knives!
It's 1183 and we're all barbarians!"

KATHARINE HEPBURN
AS ELEANOR OF AQUITAINE IN *THE LION IN WINTER*

THE GRADUATE (1967)

STARS ....Dustin Hoffman, Anne Bancroft, Katharine Ross

DIRECTOR ....Mike Nichols

WRITERS ....Calder Willingham, Buck Henry,
....based on the novel by Charles Webb

ACADEMY AWARDS ....Best Director,
....plus six nominations, including Best Picture

The Graduate cast a vote of confidence for the future of marriage, and suggested that while the institutions of the past may have turned out to be a façade disguising deep family dysfunction and personal unhappiness, it also suggested that just maybe, if we followed our hearts and were willing to think outside the box, we in the next generation could find a better way than our parents did. A very young Dustin Hoffman stars as Benjamin Braddock, a good boy fresh out of a good college, who doesn't have the first idea what to do with his life. And so he drifts into an affair with his girlfriend Elaine's (Katharine Ross) loose-lipped and loose-hipped mother (Anne Bancroft), the infamous Mrs. Robinson of Simon and Garfunkel fame , who looks like she is living her own interpretation of the ladies-who-lunch on a loop. Through Mrs. Robinson's eyes, Ben witnesses at close range the personal cost of keeping up appearances, and remaining in control. Scared straight by Mrs. Robinson's unbridled appetites, Ben stops the institution of marriage dead in its tracks and steals the bride off the top of the wedding cake. He and Elaine board a bus for parts unknown, riding hand in hand toward the emotional new frontier, armed with a modern sense of equality between the sexes, and independence from the old-fashioned brand of disappointment and regret. What is ironic, in retrospect, is that for all of Ben and Elaine's teen spirit, it is only Mrs. Robinson who is born to be wild, insisting upon going her own way, defying social convention, and refusing to ride in the back of the bus—and, as a result, is the only one who really stands a chance of redefining the institution of marriage.

LILIES OF THE FIELD (1963)

STARS .... Sidney Poitier, Lilia Skala

DIRECTOR .... Ralph Neelson

WRITER .... James Poe, based on the novel by William E. Barrett

ACADEMY AWARDS .... Best Actor, plus four nominations, including Best Picture

One of the most endearing and enduring cinematic images of the '60s is Sidney Poitier at a dinner table, surrounded by giggling nuns, teaching them to sing an old spiritual—a visual that helped destroy the image created by bigots of a frightening black man leering at white women. Yep, you can't get much more wholesome than Sidney Poitier hanging with the sisters and singing praises to the Lord.

Poitier plays Homer Smith, a traveling man in the South whose station wagon breaks down one day near a convent. The nuns' mother superior, Mother Maria (Lilia Skala), believes his appearance is a gift from God, to whom she's been praying for a handyman who can help them build a new church and do some needed repairs around the place. Smith is happy to repay her kindness at first, but somehow the obligations keep building up. For one thing, the German sisters' English isn't so good, and they feign ignorance when he protests that he's got to move on. For another thing, for all his grumbling and threats that this is the last brick he's going to lay, really it is, Smith realizes it's kind of nice to feel you're building the foundation of a genuine bond with people so different from you that you'd normally simply smile at them and move on.

This sunny little movie is a perfect mood uplifter on those days when you're wishing for some serendipity to brighten your world and remind you to overlook the small differences and connect with your fellow beings.

WORDS TO LIVE BY

"We were not put on the earth to hurry, Schmidt!"

LILIA SKALA

AS MOTHER MARIA IN *LILIES OF THE FIELD*

ROSEMARY'S BABY (1968)

STARS..Mia Farrow, John Cassavetes,
....Ruth Gordon, Sidney Blackmer

DIRECTOR ....Roman Polanski

WRITER ....Roman Polanski,
....based on the novel by Ira Levin

ACADEMY AWARDS ....Best Supporting Actress (Ruth Gordon),
....plus one nomination

Rosemary's Baby was the decade's first really creepy movie about penetration anxiety to hit the big screen, and it was also a vivid illustration of the fundamental distrust and downright fear that lay at the heart of the battle of the sexes. So we all went in droves and for weeks afterward were afraid to turn the lights out. In this frightening story about a woman adrift in a man's world, pregnancy takes center stage as the means by which a young woman is victimized by the very institutions that she turns to for comfort. Newlyweds Rosemary (Mia Farrow) and Guy Wodehouse (John Cassavetes) move into a sprawling super eight on Manhattan's Upper West Side. They are befriended by two kindly elderly neighbors, Minnie (Ruth Gordon) and Roman Castavet (Sidney Blackmer), who despite their seeming sweetness, are actually the leaders of a cult. They wind up cooperating in a conspiracy with Guy to impregnate Rosemary with the devil's spawn. Which just goes to show you, in a world governed by a corrupt patriarchy, even loving your neighbor as yourself can get you into a heap of trouble, so when it comes to creepy neighbors, sinister spouses, and OB/GYN's who prescribe herbal concoctions during pregnancy, it's probably best to get a second opinion.

THE APARTMENT (1960)

STARS ....Jack Lemmon, Shirley MacLaine, Fred MacMurray, Jack Kruschen

DIRECTOR...Billy Wilder

WRITERS ....Billy Wilder, I. A. L. Diamond

ACADEMY AWARDS ....Best Picture, Best Director, Best Screenplay (Original),
.... **plus two other awards and five nominations**

The Apartment takes a look at what the experience of men and women working side by side can do to traditional ideas of romance, and casts a suspicious eye on the possibility of peace between the sexes when life is dominated by corporate ambition and a desire for success.

Jack Lemmon stars as C. C. Baxter, an aspiring plutocrat who is working his way up from being a second assistant at New York Life Insurance by loaning his apartment to his boss for clandestine trysts after work. Trouble brews when C. C. falls in love with Fran Kubelik (Shirley MacLaine), who dreams of being married to a plutocrat and is working her way up the corporate ladder by sleeping with her married boss. This movie, which presented office infidelity as if it were a subject for situation comedies, won Best Picture and was enormously popular with audiences in the '60s who were beginning to wrestle with the question of how either side was going to win a battle of the sexes when you have to get up and go to work together in the morning.

FRAN'S FINGER FOOD

"When you're in love with a married man you shouldn't wear mascara."

· · · · · · · · · · · · · · · · ·

"Just because I wear a uniform doesn't make me a Girl Scout."

SHIRLEY MACLAINE

AS FRAN IN *THE APARTMENT*

MY FAIR LADY (1964)

STARS .... Audrey Hepburn, Rex Harrison

DIRECTOR .... George Cukor

WRITER .... Alan Jay Lerner,
.... based on the play by George Bernard Shaw

ACADEMY AWARDS .... Best Picture, Best Director,
.... Best Actor (Rex Harrison),
.... plus five other awards and four nominations

In this musical adaptation of the Pygmalion myth, Henry Higgins (Rex Harrison), a British professor of linguistics, undertakes a project designed to amuse himself and prove a point to a skeptical friend: He will take a poor Cockney girl named Eliza Doolittle (Audrey Hepburn) off the streets, teach her to speak—and act—like an upper-class lady, and pass her off as royalty. In the '60s, the idea that a few lessons in deportment could crack the cultural codes that keep us back was delightfully reassuring, and we sighed over this flick, swept up in romantic rapture.

Nowadays, however, we can't help noticing the enormous contempt Doolittle shows for Eliza: who she is, where she comes from, and what she wants from life. In his defense, he points out that he treats her no better and no worse than anyone else in her life does, and this halfhearted excuse works for our heroine, who dries her eyes quickly and sings about how she could've danced all night with her mentor. But in the post-*Feminine Mystique* era, we find it's a tad harder to be so forgiving of a bullying older man just because he can offer money and a chance to fit in with the crowd.

Watch this movie when you're in the mood for a fun and campy reminder that we gals have come a long way, baby, and we don't need to settle for egotistical saviors anymore.

A THOUSAND CLOWNS (1966)

STARS ....Jason Robards, Barbara Harris,
.... Martin Balsam, William Daniels, Barry Gordon

DIRECTOR ....Fred Coe

WRITER ....Herb Gardner, based on his play

ACADEMY AWARDS ....Best Supporting Actor (Martin Balsam),
.... plus three nominations, including Best Picture

Tempted to tune in, turn on, drop out? *A Thousand Clowns* manages to celebrate idiosyncrasy and anarchy while warning us that there's a price to be paid for unchecked hedonism, and it's usually paid by the people we love.

Former children's TV writer Murray Burns (Jason Robards) has had it with the daily grind of an office job and would prefer to spend his time waving to departed ocean liners and playing ditties on the ukulele accompanied by his ward and precocious nephew, Nicholas (Barry Gordon). However, Murray tends to repress the fact that the social services system doesn't smile kindly upon unemployed adult guardians who leave the worrying about food and bills to children. Well, it's true, Murray's brother, Arnold (Martin Balsam), who claims to have a "talent for surrender," does pop in daily to bring fresh fruit, check in on them—and gently urge Murray to at least consider getting a job again. This, however, will not be enough to keep Murray and Nick's heads above water.

Social worker Albert Amundson (William Daniels) is ready to take Nick away from this environment, but his able assistant and fiancée, Sandra Markowitz (Barbara Harris), becomes enamored of the boy and his eccentric uncle and impulsively quits her job and her commitment to Albert. She moves in with Murray and Nick and starts sewing curtains, tidying up—and gently urging Murray to get a job. Meanwhile, Nick puts on a good front for Mr. Amundson, makes arrangements to live with the lady upstairs should Murray lose custody of him—and gently urges Murray to get a job.

Can Murray let go of his need for independence and find happiness in interdependence? Can he sacrifice just a bit in order to be a part of an alternative family that cherishes and supports his eccentricity?

Back when we were discovering that love is all you need—but recognizing that someone's still going to have to put food on the table—*A Thousand Clowns* promised us security and community without our having to sacrifice a sense of adventure and joie de vivre. When you and your significant other are squabbling over the proper balance between work and play, indulge in *A Thousand Clowns* and see if it doesn't help you two meet in the middle.

THE WORLD ACCORDING TO MURRAY

"I want to be sure he knows when he's chickening out on himself.
I want him to get to know the special thing he is,
or else he won't notice it when it starts to go.
I want him to stay awake and know who the phonies are.
I want him to know how to holler and put up an argument.
I want a little more guts to show before I can let him go.
I want to be sure he sees all the wild possibilities.
I want him to know it's worth all the trouble just to give the
world a little goosing once you get the chance.
I want him to know the sneaky, subtle
reason he was born a human being and not a chair."

. . . .

"In a moment, Nick, you're going to see a horrible thing—people going to work."

JASON ROBARDS
AS MURRAY BURNS IN *A THOUSAND CLOWNS*

Sandra (Barbara Harris): Well, Murray, just sort of to
return to reality for a moment—
Murray (Jason Robards): I'll only go as a tourist.
FROM *A THOUSAND CLOWNS*

WEST SIDE STORY (1961)

STARS .... Natalie Wood, Richard Beymer,
.... Rita Moreno, George Chakiris

DIRECTORS .... Jerome Robbins, Robert Wise

WRITERS .... Jerome Robbins, Arthur Laurents, Ernest Lehman,
.... based on the play *Romeo and Juliet* by William Shakespeare

ACADEMY AWARDS .... Best Picture, Best Director,
.... Best Supporting Actor (George Chakiris),
.... Best Supporting Actress (Rita Moreno),
.... Best Musical Score, plus five other awards and one nomination

This musical interpretation of *Romeo and Juliet*, set in New York City, is an entertaining and accessible exploration into gang warfare and racial violence that provides a poignant plea for sanity.

Natalie Woods plays Maria, a lovely Puerto Rican princess in a plain cotton dress, who wants to be a good girl and obey her paternalistic brother Bernardo's (George Chakiris) command to stay away from white boys who can only spell trouble. But one night, Maria goes to a dance in a school gym and meets up with a white boy named Tony (Richard Beymer), and the two fall madly in love. Tony tries to convince his gang that the Puerto Ricans aren't such a threat, and Bernardo's girlfriend, Anita (Rita Moreno), attempts to unite the star-crossed lovers. Meanwhile, the Sharks and the Jets slink through alleyways, snapping their fingers, sneering at authority figure Officer Krupke, and engaging in choreographed rumbles to the wailing sounds of discordant modern jazz. Alas, Tony's, Maria's, and Anita's call for understanding gets lost as the winds of fear and prejudice gather into a powerful storm that sweeps through the streets and leaves in its wake a Shakespearean tragedy.

West Side Story's bittersweet and haunting tale of love and death reminds us of how powerfully destructive the forces of ignorance and bigotry can be.

OLIVER! (1968)

STARS .... Ron Moody, Shani Wallis, Oliver Reed, Mark Lester, Jack Wild

DIRECTOR .... Carol Reed

WRITER .... Vernon Harris, based on the novel by Charles Dickens

ACADEMY AWARDS .... Best Picture, Best Director,
.... plus three other awards and six nominations

It is interesting that the '60s felt such a kinship with nineteenth-century England. Perhaps the period resonated for us because, like the '60s, it was a time of great division between rich and poor, and it allowed us to look at our own problems through the fairy-tale lens of Hollywood history. Or maybe, despite our raised consciousness, we secretly still longed for a big production number with lavish costumes, one that would set our toes to tapping while it preached the new morality of the middle class.

Oliver! was one of the last big musicals to come out of Hollywood in the '60s. It was the Best Picture of 1968, and a whole generation of American preteens (ourselves included) fell head over heels for Oliver (Mark Lester), who spends the whole movie looking for love, and eventually, despite a cruel and unforgiving world, finds it. Along the way, he encounters the usual array of colorful characters that populated the British period movies of the time. There's the corrupt ringleader with a heart of gold, Fagin (Ron Moody), who tries to profit from Oliver's misfortune; the surrogate mom, Nancy (Shani Wallace), who sacrifices her life for Oliver's; and a rakish bad boy called the Artful Dodger (Jack Wild) for the little girls whose sensibilities ran more toward John Lennon than Paul McCartney. The only dark

OSCAR FUN FACTS

In 1967, the Academy did away with separate Best Costume Design, Best Art Direction, and Best Cinematography awards for color and black-and-white films, since black-and-white films were becoming a rarity.

cloud in the whole movie is the dreaded Bill Sykes (Oliver Reed), who reminded us that not all endings are as happy as Oliver's. *Oliver!* was enormously popular with audiences who wanted to believe that we would all find our way home eventually, and despite the wickedness of the world, would discover an unconditional love and a lasting peace.

HOME, HOME ON THE RANGE

In the '60s, when we were forging new emotional and political paths without a map, even our Westerns began to take on the contours of our social frontier.

MIDNIGHT COWBOY (1969)

STARS	Jon Voight, Dustin Hoffman
DIRECTOR	John Schlesinger
WRITER	Waldo Salt, based on the novel by James Leo Herlihy
ACADEMY AWARDS	Best Picture, Best Director, Best Screenplay (Adapted), plus four nominations

Joe Buck (Jon Voight), a transplanted cowboy in the urban frontier, quits his day job in Dallas and travels to the Big Apple with dreams of fame and fortune as a high-paid male gigolo. Unfortunately, downscale cowboy chic is out that year, and eventually Joe has to admit that no matter how he may have dazzled the yellow roses of Texas, he can't get arrested on the streets of New York. Down on his heels and sleeping in a box, Joe hooks up with a tubercular bargain-basement pimp named Ratso Rizzo (Dustin Hoffman), who promises to help him hook up and then steals Joe Buck's wallet. But somehow, Ratso's betrayal brings out the real cowboy in Joe Buck: He goes in pursuit of Ratso and demands satisfaction. And ironically, he gets it. Because Ratso and Joe Buck turn out to be soul mates, brothers in crime, two outlaws on the urban frontier, who remind us that even in a cruel and uninhabitable urban badland, roses grow when there is love.

"I only get carsick on boats."

JON VOIGHT

AS JOE BUCK IN *MIDNIGHT COWBOY*

"You want the word on that brother-and-sister act: Hansel's a fag and
Gretel's got the hots for herself, so who cares, right?
Load up on the salami."

·····················

"Frankly, you're beginning to smell, and for a stud in New York,
that's a handicap."

DUSTIN HOFFMAN

AS RATSO RIZZO IN *MIDNIGHT COWBOY*

BUTCH CASSIDY AND THE SUNDANCE KID (1969)

STARS .... Paul Newman, Robert Redford, Katharine Ross

DIRECTOR .... George Roy Hill

WRITER .... William Goldman

ACADEMY AWARDS .... Best Screenplay (Original)
.... plus three more awards and three nominations, including Best Picture

This top-grossing Western of all time took the Robin Hood morality of the late
'60s and planted it right in the heart of the American frontier. Butch Cassidy (Paul
Newman) and the Sundance Kid (Robert Redford, in his even-hotter-than-Brad-
Pitt phase) six-shot their way into America's heart as a lovable pair of best buddies
who spend their downtime in some kind of frontier interpretation of a Woodstock

commune, funded by the purloined purses of the rich and backed up by a sentimental Burt Bacharach score. Needless to say, we fell in love with this movie, and with the lovable outlaws who represented our ideal vision of the American cowboy: really good hair, piercing blue eyes, a devastating smile, an aversion to violence, and a complete and total disregard for anyone's laws but his own.

WORDS OF WISDOM FROM
THE WILD WILD WEST

"Kid, the next time I say, 'Let's go someplace like Bolivia,'
let's go someplace like Bolivia."

. . . .

"Don't ever hit your mother with a shovel.
It will leave a dull impression on her mind."

PAUL NEWMAN
AS BUTCH CASSIDY IN *BUTCH CASSIDY AND THE SUNDANCE KID*

THE PRIME OF MISS JEAN BRODIE (1969)

STARS .... Maggie Smith, Pamela Franklin, Celia Johnson, ... Robert Stephens, Jane Carr, Diane Grayson, Gordon Jackson

DIRECTOR .... Ronald Neame

WRITER .... Jay Presson Allen, ... based on his play, based on the novel by Muriel Spark

ACADEMY AWARDS .... Best Actress (Maggie Smith), plus one nomination

Maggie Smith has made a career out of playing iconoclasts who speak in an arch tone to their inferiors (read: everyone). And in this seminal performance, she brings to life a character whom we can't help loving for her zest and adventurousness, but who learns the hard way that getting along means tempering your enthusiasm for extreme behaviors—particularly if you're low on the totem pole at a Scottish girls' boarding school.

Miss Jean Brodie (Maggie Smith) dazzles her pupils with her forthright opinions about everything from art to literature and how far one can open a window or roll up one's sleeves before committing the sin of vulgarity. And she's never been at a loss for male admirers, although she has little patience for the convention of monogamy, much less marriage. She is in her prrrrrime, devoted to her girls, and declares, "I do not intend to devote my prrrrrime to petrification."

However, there is a difference between petrification and reckless behavior. Miss Brodie is at last confronted with the consequences of refusing to rein in her free spirit even to the slightest degree, cautioning all of us to use a modicum of common sense in our rebellions.

Watch this one when you're feeling oppressed by the need to conform and to get in touch with your own need to live life fully and passionately.

THE WORLD ACCORDING TO MISS JEAN BRRRRRODIE

"Color enlivens the spirit, does it not?"

. . . .

"Little girls! I am in the business of putting old heads on young shoulders,
and all my pupils are the crème de la crème.
Give me a girl at an impressionable age and she is mine for life."

. . . .

"Oh, chrysanthemums. Such . . . serviceable flowers."

MAGGIE SMITH

AS JEAN BRODIE IN *THE PRIME OF MISS JEAN BRODIE*

GUESS WHO'S COMING TO DINNER? (1967)

STARS ....Katharine Hepburn, Spencer Tracy,
....Sidney Poitier, Katharine Houghton,
....Cecil Kellaway, Beah Richards, Roy Glenn

DIRECTOR ....Stanley Kramer

WRITER...William Rose

ACADEMY AWARDS ....Best Actress (Katharine Hepburn),
....Best Screenplay (Original),
....plus eight nominations, including Best Picture

In the winter after the Summer of Love, it made sense that we embraced a movie featuring two nice middle-class white parents who discover that their daughter is engaged to a man from a nice middle-class black family, ending with an "all you need is love" theme.

To add a little drama before that inevitable Beatlesque conclusion, Spencer Tracy takes a turn as the somewhat cantankerous Matt Drayton, who suddenly learns that his little girl is bringing to dinner not only a black man—or is it a Negro man?—but also that this black man is her fiancé (Sidney Poitier). The groom's parents (Beah Richards and Roy Glenn) are somewhat taken aback by the news as well, and are concerned that the two "kids" will face prejudice, but it's Matt who inspires worry in the hearts of his wife (Katharine Hepburn) and daughter (Katharine Houghton, Hepburn's real-life niece). Indeed, Mrs. Drayton gets a chance to angrily demand that her husband give the young couple his blessing before Matt launches into an earnest, honest monologue about how love can conquer all and these two youngsters are gonna be able to withstand bigotry and any other challenges they will face. Talk about the perfect Give Peace Among the Races a Chance Movie! Watch it when you're despairing, and reconnect with the belief that we can all break bread together at the table of brotherhood.

TO KILL A MOCKINGBIRD (1962)

STARS ....Gregory Peck, John Megna, Robert Duvall, Mary Badham, Phillip Alford

DIRECTOR ....Robert Mulligan

WRITER ....Horton Foote, based on the novel by Harper Lee

ACADEMY AWARDS ....Best Actor (Gregory Peck),
....Best Screenplay (Adapted),
.... plus one other award and five nominations, including Best Picture

Is there any character in the history of movies more beloved than Atticus Finch, as played by Gregory Peck? He always does the right thing, speaks up against prejudice, defends a black man in the Deep South accused of raping a white woman, and insists that his children hold their heads high no matter what others may say about them or their father.

We see Atticus through the eyes of his daughter, Scout (Mary Badham), who is too innocent to understand why everyone can't just get along. She even unknowingly stops a lynching when she cheerfully greets, by name, one of the men in the mob and asks after his daughter who happens to be her playmate. Confronted with the reality that they ought to be making their children proud instead of behaving like hoodlums, the crowd disperses. And taught by her father not to judge people before she knows them, the sweet-natured Scout brings a recluse, Boo Radley, back into the light of day and into the community, while her father gives hope to the local black folks that if they stick together and have faith, someday they won't face cruel injustice.

When you could use some reassurance that even at the darkest times, there are still good people willing to stand up against those who are acting out of fear and hatred, immerse yourself in the world of *To Kill a Mockingbird*. And stand up—because Atticus Finch is passing.

TOM JONES (1963)

STARS .... Albert Finney, Susannah York

DIRECTOR .... Tony Richardson

WRITER .... John Osborne, based on the novel by Henry Fielding

ACADEMY AWARDS .... Best Picture, Best Director,
.... Best Screenplay (Adapted), Best Music Score, plus six nominations

• •

Tom Jones was an enormously successful film, and took Best Picture in the fateful year of 1963, when movie audiences were no doubt grappling with some severe shocks to the national psyche in the wake of the Kennedy assassination. In contrast to the country's heavy heart, this movie is a frivolous period romp that transformed the bawdy peccadilloes of eighteenth-century Londoners into a '60s-style free-for-all that foreshadowed the Summer of Love, and never once even hinted that there might be a price to pay for thoughtless hedonism.

Tom Jones (Albert Finney), a foundling and presumably a bastard, is left on a doorstep for the first passerby to happen upon. But fate smiles on Tom that day, and he is taken into the home of an English gentleman and raised as a nobleman's son. Tom has no regard for his good fortune, however, and no understanding that fate could have frowned on him, too, just as easily as it smiled. And so he squanders his good fortune and becomes an uncontrollable and licentious youth, which means he basically runs around having

a great time and doesn't care who knows about it. As a consequence, Tom is turned out of his benefactor's home and separated from his true love, the indefatigable Sophie (Susannah York), to whom he vows to return . . . eventually.

Tom Jones was a carefree Candide for a difficult time, a Kennedy-style optimist who believed that he was living in the best of all possible worlds, despite overwhelming evidence to the contrary. Tom didn't see anything wrong with having a good time in the moment, and didn't worry about the consequences. In a time of political and cultural seismic shifts, *Tom Jones* was like a cleansing breath, and a welcome escape into a world where there were no consequences, and the only thing that mattered was that it felt good.

OSCAR FUN FACTS

Among the classic '60s songs that did not win Best Song from a Motion Picture, despite qualifying for that award, were:

"What's New, Pussycat"
"The Look of Love"
"Alfie"
"Georgy Girl"

And these songs, which weren't even nominated:

"To Sir with Love"
"Mrs. Robinson"
"Help!"
"A Hard Day's Night"
"Yellow Submarine"

IN THE HEAT OF THE NIGHT (1967)

STARS .... Sidney Poitier, Rod Steiger, Lee Grant

DIRECTOR .... Norman Jewison

WRITER .... Stirling Silliphant, based on the novel by John Ball

ACADEMY AWARDS .... Best Picture, Best Actor (Rod Steiger),
.... Best Screenplay (Adapted), plus two other awards and two nominations

· ·

Getting along requires mutual respect, and if ever there were a classic movie moment about the power of dignity to move the heart and mind of one's enemy, it's in this flick, when Sidney Poitier tells Rod Steiger in no uncertain terms that where he comes from, "They call me Mister Tibbs."

Steiger plays Gillespie, a big-bellied, white-southern-sheriff stereotype who smacks gum, drawls, and spits at the very thought of the big city. But when Philadelphia homicide detective Virgil Tibbs (Sidney Poitier) shows up at Gillespie's office one hot, lazy summer night, having been arrested basically for walking while black, Gillespie puts aside his preconceived notions about this Tibbs fellow. Realizing that Tibbs is a far better investigator than he is, Gillespie grudgingly humbles himself to ask him not to hightail it back East on the next train and shake the dust of this Podunkville off his shoes, but instead help Gillespie solve a murder. Tibbs reluctantly agrees, and as he starts turning over stones, Gillespie watches in admiration, suddenly seeing that he's not so different from Tibbs after all. For his part, Tibbs begins to respect Gillespie's awareness of the local culture, his bravery in keeping Tibbs from harm, and his willingness to put being a good cop ahead of his own pride. Indeed, the two men have a lot in common, for they are both proud, ambitious, and good at police work—although from what we see, Tibbs is clearly the superior when it comes to *GQ* eloquence and proper verb conjugation. By the time Tibbs heads home, it's obvious he has forever altered Gillespie's ideas about black men, just as Gillespie has altered Tibbs's ideas about seemingly incorrigible bigots.

Watch this movie when you need inspiration to be your highest self and connect with those who aren't quite as far along in their personal growth as you are.

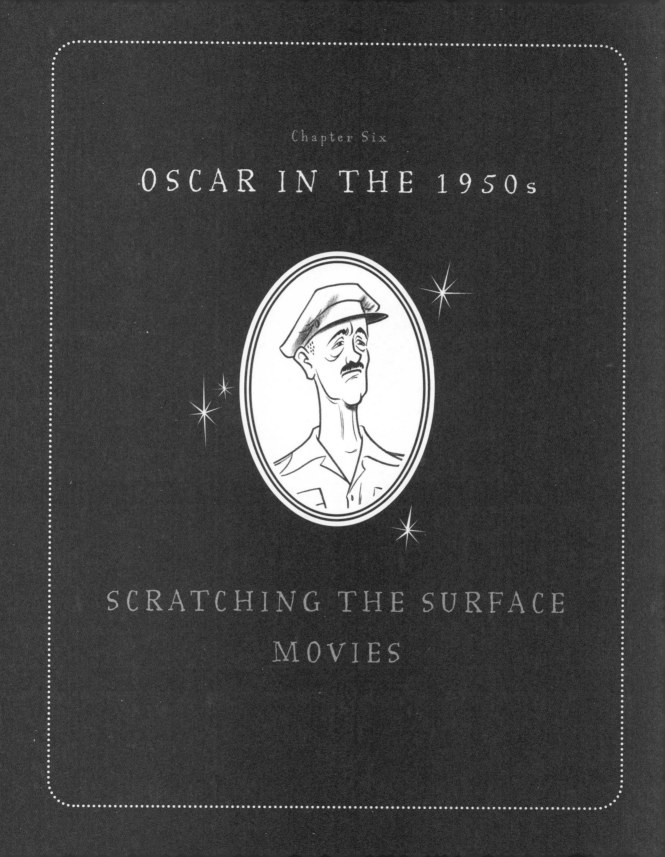

Chapter Six

OSCAR IN THE 1950s

SCRATCHING THE SURFACE

MOVIES

Oh, those golden '50s, when we were all munching on burgers and fries but no one had a weight problem, we were certain that Senator McCarthy would get rid of those nasty communists, and all of us throughout the land lived in a perpetual state of cheerful consumerism. Well, okay, maybe not. Following a decade of war and deprivation, spiraling inflation, and the sobering realization that we now had the power to destroy ourselves, many Americans were quick to pop a happy pill and deny reality, as some of the breezier movies of the era showed. And yet, despite all the fluffy Hollywood fare in theaters, Academy Awards were very often presented to movies that reflected the realization that gleeful delusion wasn't as effective a defense mechanism as we'd all hoped it would be. These Scratching the Surface Movies of the '50s feature butchers, army colonels, and French schoolgirls who feel pressured to spend their energy keeping up appearances but find the courage to deal instead with far more weighty matters. These films challenge us to look beneath the surface of our own existence, and promise that when we take off the rose-colored glasses—and the sequined tutus—we'll be relieved of the heavy burden of denial at last.

FROM HERE TO ETERNITY (1953)

STARS .... Burt Lancaster, Montgomery Clift, Deborah Kerr,
.... Donna Reed, Frank Sinatra, Philip Ober, Ernest Borgnine

DIRECTOR .... Fred Zinneman

WRITER .... Daniel Taradash, based on the novel by James Jones

ACADEMY AWARDS .... Best Picture, Best Director,
.... Best Supporting Actor (Frank Sinatra),
.... Best Supporting Actress (Donna Reed),
.... Best Screenplay, plus three other awards and five nominations

· ·

Set in Oahu in the summer and fall of 1941, this cinematic countdown to Pearl Harbor showcases the lives of military men and women who wrestle with the boredom, isolation, and excruciating emotional trivia of their base-camp reality, without any idea of the impending doom looming behind the scenes. Nothing in this movie behaves like it should. Prewitt (Montgomery Clift) is a boxer who won't box, Captain Holmes (Burt Lancaster) is a leader who won't lead, Mrs. Holmes is an ideal officer's wife with a fidelity problem, and Maggio (Frank Sinatra) doesn't sing even once. Hovering over their tawdry dramas, steamy surf scenes, and petty political struggles is the approaching attack on Pearl Harbor, destined to change the world forever. For wartime audiences only a generation removed from Pearl Harbor and already dabbling in Korea, this movie must have been a sobering reminder that life is short, and war is hell, so it's best to pick your battles wisely.

MILITARY MANTRAS

"That's what I like about you, Sergeant: You have confidence.
It's also what I dislike about you."

DEBORAH KERR

AS KAREN HOLMES IN *FROM HERE TO ETERNITY*

ON THE WATERFRONT (1954)

STARS .... Marlon Brando, Eva Marie Saint, Karl Malden, Lee J. Cobb, Rod Steiger

DIRECTOR .... Elia Kazan

WRITER .... Budd Schulberg, based on articles by Malcolm Johnson

ACADEMY AWARDS .... Best Picture, Best Director, Best Actor (Marlon Brando), Best Supporting Actress (Eva Marie Saint), Best Story and Screenplay, plus three more awards and four nominations

Marlon Brando stars as Terry Malloy, a low-rent prizefighter who has long since been counted out after agreeing to take a dive for the Mob. His reward was a cushy job on the waterfront working for crime boss Johnny Friendly. In his spare time, Terry cares for the pigeons in his rooftop aviary, hangs out with the boys down by the docks, and broods over what might have been. When his friend Joey Doyle is murdered for cooperating with Crime Commission investigators, Terry must step back into the ring in a prizefight for his own soul, and decide once again whether he is a contender, or a bum.

This is what is happening on the surface of this movie, but underneath, Elia Kazan, who turned in his colleagues to the House Un-American Activities Commission, is pleading with his community for understanding. In Terry's ham-fisted yet delicately sensitive struggle to do the right thing, we can see the film director's own pain, and the pain of every man who believes that he has to name names in order to save lives. In addition, Marlon Brando's groundbreaking performance broke through the mannered style of American acting, and gave audiences, for perhaps the first time, a gritty, visceral, and naturalistic picture of what a man like Terry Malloy has to go through, and how grim real life can be. This movie was an Academy and box-office smash hit, so clearly all of us in the '50s, immersed as we were in a world that valued appearances over reality, could still relate to the story of a man who risked everything to tell the truth.

UNDER THE BOARDWALK

"You think you're God Almighty, but you know what you are?
You're a cheap, lousy, dirty, stinkin' mug!
And I'm glad what I done to you, ya hear that? I'm glad what I done!"

• • • • • • • • • • • • • • • •

"You don't understand. I coulda had class. I coulda been a contender.
I coulda been someone, Charley, instead of a bum,
which is what I am, let's face it. I'm a bum."

MARLON BRANDO
AS TERRY MALLOY IN *ON THE WATERFRONT*

COME BACK, LITTLE SHEBA (1952)

STARS .... **Shirley Booth, Burt Lancaster, Terry Moore, Richard Jaeckel**

DIRECTOR .... **Daniel Mann**

WRITER .... **Ketti Frings, based on the play by William Inge**

ACADEMY AWARDS .... **Best Actress (Shirley Booth), plus two nominations**

. . . .

This small domestic drama, which takes place entirely within the home of an aging couple, is a simple but eloquent plea for bringing the pain of the past to the surface and working it through instead of hiding behind a big smile or inside a bottle of scotch.

When a college student, Marie (Terry Moore), rents a room in their home, Doc Delaney (Burt Lancaster) and his wife, Lola (Shirley Booth), find it increasingly difficult to ignore the dark secrets and unspoken disappointments that have lain between them for years. Doc had married the beautiful and vivacious Lola after they discovered she was pregnant, but she lost the baby, never to have another, and Doc—who had to become a chiropractor instead of a doctor to support his wife—soon began drinking away his feelings of anger, resentment, and frustration. Lola transferred her affections to her little dog, Sheba, who has disappeared, along with Lola's youth, figure, and sex life. Lola starts spying on Marie and her hot-blooded suitors, fondly recalling her more passionate days, while Doc seethes, watching the young men traveling the same road he did. By the end of the movie, it all comes to a head as Lola and Doc have to face what they've been avoiding all these years if they're to have any hope of true intimacy.

With its attention to the nuances of human interaction, and Shirley Booth's powerful portrayal of a woman trying to put a brave spin on her pain, *Come Back, Little Sheba* remains a compelling film. Watch it when you want to talk about difficult emotions that have been buried for far too long, and see if it doesn't inspire you to stop pretending everything's just hunky-dory.

12 ANGRY MEN (1957)

STARS .... Henry Fonda, Lee J. Cobb,
.... Ed Begley Sr., Jack Klugman

DIRECTOR .... Sidney Lumet

WRITER .... Reginald Rose

ACADEMY AWARDS .... None.
.... Nominated for Best Picture, Best Director,
.... and Best Screenplay (Adapted).

Hey, we loved *The Bridge on the River Kwai*, but couldn't they have given *12 Angry Men* at least one of the three awards it was nominated for? This is an enduring movie about the American criminal justice system that can still inspire a post–McCarthy, post–Warren Commission, post–Watergate investigation, post–Clinton–impeachment, post–OJ America to believe that really, no kidding, there's hope that the whole truth will come out and justice will be served. Henry Fonda plays Mr. Davis, better known as simply Juror Number 8, trying to do his job and look under the surface of the prosecution's case (and past the dismal presentation by the defense) to determine whether a poor troubled teenager from the South Bronx actually knifed his father to death in a fit of rage or not. The rest of the jurors, particularly Number 3 (Lee J. Cobb), would just as soon pronounce the kid guilty and get out of the stifling hot pressure cooker of a New York City juror's room in the dog days of summer.

This movie promises that a nice cool splash of water on the face, a working fan, and one man who truly believes in the American way can turn the tide of injustice.

SAYONARA (1957)

STARS ....Marlon Brando, Patricia Owens,
....James Garner, Martha Scott, Miiko Taka,
....Red Buttons, Ricardo Montalban, Miyoshi Umeki

DIRECTOR...Joshua Logan

WRITER...Paul Osborn, based on the novel by James A. Michener

ACADEMY AWARDS ....Best Supporting Actor (Red Buttons),
....Best Supporting Actress (Miyoshi Umeki),
....plus two other awards and six nominations, including Best Picture

The problem with war, as the U.S. military has figured out over the years, is that the momentum of hate keeps getting interrupted by the power of love, which is highly disruptive to military discipline and the need to keep foreigners looking like inferiors. In this movie, based on true cases involving armed forces overseas, several military men stationed in Japan during the Korean War fall in love with local women despite having been told they are not supposed to fraternize with, much less love and marry, the girls of their dreams, under penalty of having their U.S. citizenship stripped and their military benefits yanked. Ah, but love isn't conquered so easily.

Airman Joe Kelly (Red Buttons) is one of several problematic soldiers that the Air Force wants disciplined before things get out of hand, and his superior officer, a southern good ol' boy named Major Lloyd Gruver (Marlon Brando), does his diplomatic best to convince Kelly not to keep carrying on with this, uh, "slant-eyed runt" he's been dating. To his cred-

OSCAR'S RED CARPET:
PROUD TO BE ME

Accepting the award for Best Supporting Actress for *Sayonara*, Miyoshi Umeki scurried up to the podium wearing a traditional silk Japanese kimono and sandals.

it, Kelly doesn't knock Gruver across the room for his racist comment, nor does he toss back at him the "helpful" pamphlets Gruver gave him, which have titles like "Things You Are Required to Know and Do Before Marrying Orientals" and "But—Will Your Family Accept Her?" Instead, Kelly vows to stay loyal to his girl, Katsumi (Miyoshi Umeki), and even marry her someday. And Gruver, to his great surprise, discovers he respects Kelly's decision, and before you know it, he too is falling for a local woman—a Kabuki actress named Hana-ogi (Miiko Taka). Gruver learns her language and begins to communicate, the walls of prejudice begin to tumble, and the U.S. Air Force starts getting very nervous, given that Gruver's the guy who is supposed to keep all the other men from being seen in the company of local women.

In an era when many Americans were just beginning to wake up to the realities of prejudice, *Sayonara* encouraged us to open our minds and hearts, learn a little more, and stop giving in to fear under the guise of "Well, it's always been this way." Watch it when you're in the mood to see ignorance, bigotry, and institutional racism eradicated in 147 minutes.

ALL ABOUT EVE (1950)

STARS .... **Bette Davis, Anne Baxter,**
.... **George Sanders, Celeste Holm, Marilyn Monroe**

DIRECTOR AND .... **Joseph Mankiewicz**

WRITER .... **Joseph Mankiewicz, based on the story** *The Wisdom of Eve* **by Mary Orr**

ACADEMY AWARDS .... **Best Picture, Best Director,**
.... **Best Supporting Actor, Best Screenplay,**
.... **plus two other awards and eight nominations**

· ·

This movie held the record for the most nominations in Oscar history until *Titanic* came along, and it's interesting, given the movie's subject matter, that Oscar staged a real battle of the divas where *All About Eve* was concerned. All four actresses were nominated for Academy Awards, and none of them won, but we are left with a timeless classic about the deceptive nature of appearances and the comforting knowledge that even Broadway stars get the blues.

Bette Davis stars as Margo Channing, one of the brightest lights on the Broadway stage, whose signature fire and music has temporarily turned into a tin kazoo and a couple of sparklers. And so Margo does what many sputtering stars have done before her: She gets herself a groupie. Eve (Anne Baxter) idolizes Margo, and is content to carry her petticoats to the laundry and organize Margo's social calendar in exchange for the privilege of being close to her favorite star. But Eve, who appears like an adoring kitten on the surface, is actually a big-game predator with very large claws, who almost manages to take down Margo in an attempt to feed her insatiable appetite for fame and fortune.

Fortunately, in the nick of time, Margo is able to prove that she's a star inside and out, see beyond her own illusions, and discover that what she wants has been right there in front of her all along: friends who love her and a husband to grow old with. In hindsight, this was a somewhat convenient message for a society looking to nudge women out of the workplace, but it also reassures us that maturity and substance will win out over beautiful appearances every time.

BETTE BITES

"Bill's 32. He looks 32.
He looked it five years ago;
he'll look it twenty years from now.
I hate men."

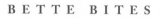

"You are in a beehive, pal. Didn't you know?
We are all busy little bees, full of stings,
making honey day and night. Aren't we, honey?"

BETTE DAVIS

AS MARGO CHANNING, IN *ALL ABOUT EVE*

MARTY (1955)

STARS..Ernest Borgnine, Betsy Blair, Esther Minciotti

DIRECTOR...Delbert Mann

WRITER...Paddy Chayefsky, based on his play

ACADEMY AWARDS..Best Picture, Best Actor, Best Director,
....Best Screenplay, plus four nominations

· ·

In the marriage-happy '50s, even guys felt the pressure to get hitched as soon as possible, lest the neighbors start publicly berating them for not conforming to the social norm and marching in line with the smug marrieds. Here's an unadorned and modest movie about a regular Joe who bravely bucks the pressure to please everyone but himself.

It's Saturday night, and though rough-faced butcher Marty (Ernest Borgnine) longs for his soul mate, he's spent far too many Saturday nights trolling the Stardust Ballroom to face the heartache of rejection yet again this weekend. Despite feeling that he's just a fat, ugly little man, somehow Marty musters up the courage to follow his mother's (Esther Minciotti) advice to launch one more expedition into the "meet" market. To his great surprise, Marty hooks up with a nice girl, Clara (Betsy Blair), whose love woes match his own: She's been dumped by her blind date because he thought she was "a dog." Marty is horrified at this cru-

NANCY'S MOMENTOUS MINUTIAE: THAT'S MY WIFE YOU'RE MESSING WITH

Actress Betsy Blair, who had been active in Screen Actors Guild politics in the '40s, was blackballed during the McCarthy era in the '50s. The only reason she was able to be cast in *Marty* was because her husband, dancer Gene Kelly, told his bosses at MGM that he would stop working if they didn't let her appear in the movie.

elty and escorts her out of the ballroom to take her on a magical midnight tour of the streets and diners of the Bronx. But when daylight comes, can Marty bravely follow his heart instead of the voices of his friends and his mother, who claim they want him to find happiness but, deep down, only want it on their terms?

This movie reassured us that we don't need lots of glamour and high production values to find happiness, and urged us to shut out the cacophony of naysayers who can't appreciate what lies deep in our hearts.

THE GREATEST SHOW ON EARTH (1952)

STARS .... Betty Hutton, Charlton Heston,
.... James Stewart, Cornel Wilde, Dorothy Lamour

DIRECTOR .... Cecil B. DeMille

WRITERS .... Fredric M. Frank, Barré Lyndon, and Theodore St. John,
.... based on a story by Fredric M. Frank, Theodore St. John, and Frank Cavett

ACADEMY AWARDS .... Best Picture,
.... Best Writing (Motion Picture Story),
.... plus three nominations

The Greatest Show on Earth is a sparkly, kitschy, Technicolor extravaganza with the theme "The show must go on." It features a clown who is really—*shhh!*—a murderer on the run from the cops (James Stewart); a gruff circus operator named Brad (Charlton Heston), who's actually a softie struggling to commit to his girlfriend; an oily trapeze artist (Cornel Wilde), who seems to be a womanizer but is secretly looking for marriage to that one special girl; and another trapeze artist (Betty Hutton), who flirts with disaster in the name of entertaining the masses when, in fact, her real motive is to provoke her boyfriend into being more attentive.

Amid the peanuts, the popcorn, and the midget extras, the folks in this traveling circus duke out their dramas backstage only to turn around come showtime and slap on greasepaint, turquoise sequined leotards, and great big Brownie smiles and pretend everything's going swimmingly. Of course, the performers can't always contain their real-life squabbles, and the audience collectively gasps as trapeze artists perform harebrained stunts out of spite or an elephant trainer makes a pachyderm get rough with a pretty young assistant. But when real disaster strikes—*crash! bang! boom!*—leaving the circus train demolished and Brad wounded, everyone puts aside their differences and pulls together to put on the show, over in the nearest open field. We'd like to think one of those charming showgirl extras called 911 to get some paramedics to stop by as well, to attend to the scores of bruised and bleeding. But then, this isn't a movie that sweats the messy details of plot threads.

Despite putting on its own dazzling display of bright-eyed optimism, *The Greatest Show on Earth*'s undertow about the perils of running away from confrontation reminds us that there's nothing shameful about admitting we're scared or vulnerable—or that we could use a safety net.

WOE IS ME

"Aw, Buttons, I'm all achey inside, having a man love sawdust more than me."

BETTY HUTTON

IN *THE GREATEST SHOW ON EARTH*

GIRLFRIEND TO GIRLFRIEND

"Listen, sugar, the only way that you can keep me warm
is to wrap me up in a marriage license."

DOROTHY LAMOUR

AS ANGEL IN *THE GREATEST SHOW ON EARTH*

THE BRIDGE ON THE RIVER KWAI (1957)

STARS .... Alec Guinness, William Holden, Sessue Hayakawa

DIRECTOR .... David Lean

WRITERS .... Blacklisted and thus uncredited writers Michael Wilson and Carl Foreman,
.... based on the novel *La pont de la rivière Kwai*, by Pierre Boulle

ACADEMY AWARDS .... Best Picture, Best Actor (Alec Guinness),
.... Best Director, Best Screenplay (Adapted) to Pierre Boulle,
.... plus three other awards and one nomination

· ·

Stuck in a Japanese prison camp during World War II, Colonel Nicholson (Alec Guinness) vows not to let his men lose their mental fitness or give in to despair while they are tormented daily by their captors. Thus, Nicholson announces to the troops that they will indeed follow the Japanese commander's order to build a bridge on the River Kwai, but the officers will refrain from physical labor so as to maintain the integrity of discipline in the British armed forces and keep morale high. Hey, you can put vermin in a man's gruel, but you can't make him give up the vestiges of the British class system.

Between his defiant insistence on not soiling his officer's hands, and the mere mention of that Geneva Convention thing, the Japanese are not exactly happy with Nicholson. They

> ## OSCAR'S RED CARPET:
> ## KEEPING UP APPEARANCES
>
> Pierre Boulle did not show up to the ceremonies the year that he won Best Screenplay for *The Bridge on the River Kwai*, sending Kim Novak to the podium in his stead. Considering that Boulle was a front for the blacklisted real writers of the movie, Michael Wilson and Carl Foreman, we can understand his reluctance to play along with the charade. Wilson and Foreman went uncredited for years but were posthumously awarded an Oscar for Best Screenplay in 1984, after Wilson had died (and poor Foreman died the very next day).

torture him until the resigned Brit realizes he must find a face-saving compromise that allows the bridge to be built properly, without him or the Japanese commander Colonel Saito (Sessue Hayakawa) looking bad. Everyone's happy, and the fellas put on a celebratory show (apparently, while rations are short, theater equipment and costumes are not, just like on "Gilligan's Island").

Except, of course, that Nicholson has forgotten that they're in the middle of a war, and war is messy and illogical and tends to blow up any illusions of control, along with any delusions of grandeur. The look on Nicholson's face as he comes to this realization serves as an indelible reminder that true meaning is to be found in how we embrace and approach life, and that monuments to our pride are impermanent and fragile.

GETTING DOWN TO THE NITTY-GRITTY

"Do not speak to me of rules! This is war, not a game of cricket!"

SESSUE HAYAKAWA

AS COLONEL SAITO IN *THE BRIDGE ON THE RIVER KWAI*

"You give me powders, pills, baths, injections, enemas—when all I need is love."

WILLIAM HOLDEN

AS MAJOR SHEARS IN *THE BRIDGE ON THE RIVER KWAI*

I WANT TO LIVE! (1958)

STARS .... Susan Hayward, Simon Oakland, Theodore Bikel, Virginia Vincent

DIRECTOR .... Robert Wise

WRITERS .... Nelson Gidding, Don M. Mankiewicz,
.... based on newspaper articles by Edward S. Montgomery
.... and the letters of Barbara Graham

ACADEMY AWARDS .... Best Actress (Susan Hayward), plus five nominations

At a time when even loose women wore girdles, Susan Hayward dug down deep and gave us a compelling portrait of a tough gal who refuses to see that smart suits, perfect grooming, and a matching pocketbook and shoes aren't enough to convince people of her innocence.

Simon Oakland plays a reporter who becomes fascinated by Barbara "Babs" Graham (Susan Hayward), a prostitute accused of being an accessory to murder. Sure, Mrs. Graham hangs out in jazz clubs and shimmies and shakes to bongo beats. Sure, she consorts with burglars, was locked up in reform school, passed bad checks, and has done a year's time for perjury. But "Babs" declares she's innocent, really she is. She only wants to settle down and be a housewife and take care of her baby like any woman would. She don't know nothing about that crippled dame in Burbank who turned up dead, see? So if you want to dub her the Titian Tigress to sell papers, well, go ahead, 'cause she's gettin' out of this joint.

Graham's refusal to face the seriousness of her situation, stop worrying about how tacky the prison sleepwear is, and put some more thought into how to save herself from the gas chamber is a wonderful cautionary tale about the power of prejudice. In an era where keep-

OSCAR FUN FACTS

Susan Hayward played an alcoholic character three times in the movies (*Smash Up*, *My Foolish Heart*, and *I'll Cry Tomorrow*), and each time she was nominated for an Academy Award, but didn't win until she played an accused murderess in *I Want to Live!*

ing up appearances was held at a premium, *I Want to Live!* let us enjoy watching a proud woman who refuses to tailor her image to please the masses. Even so, it warns us that people's preconceived notions sometimes stomp all over the truth.

WHAT WERE THEY THINKING?

THE QUIET MAN (1952)

STARS ....John Wayne, Maureen O'Hara

DIRECTOR ....John Ford

WRITER ....Frank S. Nugent, based on the story "Green Rushes" by Maurice Walsh

ACADEMY AWARDS ....Best Director, Best Cinematography, ...plus five nominations, including Best Picture and Best Screenplay

What could be more romantic than a rough working-class fellow from Pittsburgh winning the heart of a spirited Irish lass, tussling his way through the standard second-act conflict, until at last the emerald green fields fill with villagers cheering on his successful conquest? Well, you know, it all sounds cute on paper, but the Academy apparently missed the undertow here, or deliberately chose to ignore it. You see, while this St. Patrick's Day classic is, on the surface, just another one of those dopey and contrived romances, underneath it's a creepy tale about a gal who is happy to get shoved around by her husband. Maureen O'Hara's character, Mary Kate, is a fiery redhead, fiercely proud despite her poverty, and notorious for her independence; yet we're supposed to find it sexy and romantic when Sean (John Wayne), a newcomer from America, forces kisses on her, dismisses her concerns about losing her money and possessions if she marries him, and drags her off as a local woman offers him "a good stick to beat the lovely lady."

Even on those evenings when we are at our most mindless and ready to forgive a multitude of twisted cultural messages in the name of shallow indulgence, this one makes us less likely to sip a fruity martini and giggle than to knock back a few shots of the hard stuff and mutter about patriarchal dominance, American hegemony, and whatever happened to those great women's movies of bygone eras.

HARVEY (1950)

STARS .... James Stewart, Josephine Hull

DIRECTOR .... Henry Koster

WRITERS .... Mary Chase, Oscar Brodney, Myles Connolly,
.... based on the play by Mary Chase

ACADEMY AWARDS .... Best Supporting Actress (Josephine Hull),
.... and one nomination

· ·

While Josephine Hull's Oscar-winning performance as the nervous Veta Louise Simmons isn't remembered quite as well as Jimmy Stewart's portrayal of the amiable Elwood P. Dowd, which didn't nab him that coveted statue, their contributions to *Harvey* are so memorable that the original play continues to live on, being massacred by amateur theatrical groups all over the country year after year.

As befits an era of glossed-over dysfunction, *Harvey* reassures us that if unsettling behavior should appear in the parlors of our staid middle-class homes, we needn't worry, because, hey, we're all kinda kooky underneath. Dowager Veta Louise Simmons (Josephine Hull) understandably freaks out at the social consequences of her brother Elwood's (James Stewart) insistence that his best friend is an invisible six-foot-three-and-a-half-inch-tall rabbit named Harvey, and goes to commit Elwood to the nuthouse. But the ever-so-pleas-

NANCY'S MOMENTOUS MINUTIAE

- Though Elwood P. Dowd (James Stewart) orders up a heck of a lot of martinis for himself and his friends in *Harvey*, he never actually takes a sip of one.

- In real life, Jimmy Stewart served in the military during World War II and as a youth had been an Eagle Scout.

ant and unflappable Elwood's hallucination begins to make its own sort of sense after we hear him explain that Harvey, who appeared after Elwood's mother died and about the time Elwood reached midlife, is the kind of companion anyone can talk to, a friend who reminds us all that life isn't so bad after a couple of martinis at the local watering hole. Couldn't we all use a few stiff ones, and a pal to look out for us as we wander aimlessly through the sleepy small towns of our existences, resisting the pull of the daily grind and spending our days saying "hullo" to everyone we meet?

The tame sexual innuendos in *Harvey* haven't aged well, and its wholesome appeal makes it feel less like an invitation to indulge in some gin or rye than to pour a big glass of whole milk with Ovaltine mixed in. Nevertheless, it's a fascinating '50s fantasy that promises that gentle folk who spend their days in dive bars talking to creatures of the imagination aren't necessarily going to launch into a painful *Lost Weekend* (1945) or a raw discovery that *The Days of Wine and Roses* (1962) are over. This was a lovely little escape at a time in our history when the working man felt considerable pressure to don a gray flannel suit, hold his liquor, and keep a lid on his emotions, and a gal was expected to smile and put up a good front at all times. So when you need to get a bit loosey-goosey, shake up a few and tipple with Elwood and his pal Harvey.

REALITY AIN'T ALL IT'S CRACKED UP TO BE

"Well, I've wrestled with reality for thirty-five years, Doctor, and I'm happy to state I finally won out over it."

JAMES STEWART

AS ELWOOD P. DOWD IN *HARVEY*

"Myrtle Mae, you have a lot to learn, and I hope you never learn it."

JOSEPHINE HULL

AS VETA LOUISE SIMMONS IN *HARVEY*

SOME LIKE IT HOT (1959)

STARS .... Tony Curtis, Jack Lemmon,
.... Marilyn Monroe, George Raft,
.... Pat O'Brien, Joe E. Brown

DIRECTOR .... Billy Wilder

WRITERS .... Billy Wilder, I. A. L. Diamond,
.... based on a story by R. Thoeren and M. Logan

ACADEMY AWARDS .... Best Costume Design, plus five nominations

....

It was during the '50s that sexy Barbie debuted as a little girl's toy, Christine Jorgensen became the first transsexual surgically changed from male to female, and teenage pregnancy was at an all-time high. This all laid the foundation for us to embrace one of the funniest films ever made about *la différence*.

Forced to go undercover and get a paying job that'll take them out of town and away from some Chicago gangsters who want to rub them out, musicians Joe (Tony Curtis) and Jerry (Jack Lemmon) join an all-female band and do their best to disguise themselves as respectable, if somewhat prudish, gals. Raising the pitch of their voices, hobbling as best they can on stilettos, donning high collars to hide their bobbing Adam's apples, and giggling a lot somehow distract the girls and their chaperone from noticing the propensity of "Daphne" and "Josephine" to salivate over their band mates. Eventually, Joe/Josephine can't deny his nature, and decides to slip into yet another disguise, as a Cary Grant–esque playboy, in order to woo band mate Sugar Kane (Marilyn Monroe). But Jerry/Daphne starts discovering his feminine side. Soon, he—or is it she?—is frolicking girlishly at the beach with her best gal pals, flirting with wealthy yachtsmen, and dreaming of romance, marriage, and financial security. Well, why not?

Half a century has passed since this classic comedy about the complexity of gender was made, and yet its skewering of rigid expectations about what men and women should be attracted to and how they should behave keeps us laughing even today.

THE GIRL CAN'T HELP IT

Joe (Tony Curtis): You're not a girl! You're a guy!
Why would a guy wanna marry a guy?
Jerry as Daphne (Jack Lemmon): Security!

· · · · · · · · · · · · · · · · · ·

Joe (Tony Curtis): What are you gonna do on your honeymoon?
Jerry as Daphne (Jack Lemmon): He wants to go to the Riviera
but I kinda lean towards Niagara Falls.

FROM *SOME LIKE IT HOT*

OSCAR'S RED CARPET:
LOOKING GOOD, PART I

● At the 1950 awards ceremony, an insecure Marilyn Monroe began to cry when she discovered before going onstage to present an award that her dress was torn, apparently unaware that there were ladies present bearing needles and thread for just such a disaster.

● In the '50s, it was common for ladies picking up Academy Awards to not only wear petticoats and elbow gloves up to the podium but fur stoles as well. And in 1953, Shirley Booth picked up her award for Best Actress while wearing little white gloves and carrying a nosegay . . . which she managed not to drop when she tripped on the steps up to the stage.

GIGI (1958)

STARS .... Leslie Caron, Louis Jourdan,
.... Maurice Chevalier, Hermione Gingold, Eva Gabor, Isabel Jeans

DIRECTOR .... Vincente Minnelli

WRITER .... Alan Jay Lerner, based on the novel by Colette

ACADEMY AWARDS .... Best Picture, Best Director,
.... Best Screenplay (Adapted), plus six other awards

• •

There's nothing like a froufrou Hollywood musical to provide temporary shelter from the harsh reality of dealing with other people's expectations of how you ought to behave. And what better hideout than an enchanting Cinemascope extravaganza that pokes fun at the phony airs of upper-class French society while placating us with a reassuring promise that love always triumphs over greed, hypocrisy, and snobbery?

As our narrator, the affable Uncle Honore (Maurice Chevalier), explains, "love" rules in turn-of-the-twentieth-century Paris. In other words, as long as you keep up appearances of respect and propriety, everyone will respect your lack of marital fidelity and your lusting after schoolgirls. Remember, we're talking about the French.

Feeding into this illusion of civility is the ultimate teacher of French manners, Aunt Alicia (Isabel Jeans), who explains to her spirited and naive teenage niece, Gigi (Leslie Caron), the correct methods for nibbling finger foods and telling a dipped pearl from the genuine article. When Gigi's grandmother, Madame Alvarez (Hermione Gingold), gets it in her head to marry off the blossoming Gigi to wealthy playboy Gaston (Louis Jourdan), she teams up

with Aunt Alicia against Gaston and his Uncle Honore to negotiate the details of a mutu-
ally acceptable upper-class Parisian match. Alas, as they bicker, poor Gigi—caught in the
tangle of complex social interrelations—is in danger of losing her innocent charm. But if her
guileless nature is corrupted, will Gaston still love her? Not to worry—plenty of creatively
rhymed songs and geography-defying carriage rides through the sights of Paris help everyone work it out perfectly.

This delightful movie, which points out that *la différence* can be very large indeed, is the
perfect antidote to courtship woes, promising that you can get past complex social rituals and
find true love and loyalty.

THE COLLECTIVE WISDOM OF KNOW-IT-ALLS

"Without knowledge of jewelry, my dear Gigi, a woman is lost."

ISABEL JEANS
AS AUNT ALICIA IN *GIGI*

"College girls are one step from the street, I tell you.
My son Joseph wife, she type on the typewriter. One step from the street!"

AUGUSTA CIOLLI
AS AUNT CATHERINE IN *MARTY*

✦ WARNING LABEL ✦

Best keep a heavy object in your lap while watching *Gigi* or you may just float away
on its gentle breeze of unreality.

BEN-HUR (1959)

STARS .... Charlton Heston, Hugh Griffith, Jack Hawkins, Stephen Boyd,
.... Martha Scott, Cathy O'Donnell, Tony Curtis

DIRECTOR .... William Wyler

WRITERS .... Karl Tunberg, Maxwell Anderson, Christopher Fry, Gore Vidal,
.... based on the novel by Lew Wallace

ACADEMY AWARDS .... Best Picture, Best Actor (Charlton Heston), Best Supporting Actor
.... (Hugh Griffith), Best Director, plus seven other awards and one nomination

• •

This Oscar heavyweight stars Charlton "NRA" Heston and was originally subtitled *The Story of the Christ*, so it's not too hard to figure out what we were responding to when we went in droves to the movie theaters to watch a biblical pageant movie about a Jewish slave turned vigilante.

William Wyler, who was Cecil B. DeMille's assistant, took a cue from DeMille's *The Ten Commandments* and cast Charlton Heston as Judah Ben-Hur, a Jewish prince who is cast into slavery by his Roman ex–best friend Messala (Stephen Boyd), and returns to exact his revenge and wash the land clean of the Romans. Many chariot races and gladiator battles ensue, followed by the crucifixion of Christ, which inspires him to put down his sword.

This was the most expensive movie made in Hollywood up to its time, and it could have turned out to be Charlton Heston's *Cleopatra*, which bankrupted Fox. But the Academy and the public were ripe for a big-screen biblical epic, complete with vaguely homoerotic love scenes between a barely postpubescent Tony Curtis and Charlton Heston in a loincloth, the latter appearing to be wholly unaware of the subtext. The first movie to win eleven Oscars, it also made $10 million at the box office. Mel Gibson was paying attention.

REEL TO REAL

• Paul Newman was offered the role of Judah Ben-Hur but turned it down because he said he didn't have the legs to wear a tunic.

• Burt Lancaster claimed he turned down the role of Judah Ben-Hur because he "didn't like the violent morals in the story."

THE DIARY OF ANNE FRANK (1959)

STARS .... Millie Perkins, Joseph Schildkraut,
.... Shelley Winters, Diane Baker, Gusti Huber

DIRECTOR .... George Stevens

WRITERS .... Frances Goodrich, Albert Hackett,
.... based on the diary of Anne Frank

ACADEMY AWARDS .... Best Supporting Actress (Shelley Winters),
.... plus two other awards
.... and five nominations, including Best Picture

Not everyone has what it takes to be a beacon of dignity in the face of danger, and as the pampered and fretting Mrs. Van Daan, Shelley Winters reminds us that one can be brave and admirable and yet definitely have one's whiny moments.

To be honest, Mrs. Van Daan has a lot of whiny moments, but how can we blame her? Shut up in a tiny space with her husband, her son, another family—the Franks—and a dentist friend for years while hiding out from the Nazis, Mrs. Van Daan can't help complaining about the lack of food and the children's annoying behavior, and going on and on about how nice life used to be. While Anne (Millie Perkins) struggles not to resent her seemingly perfect sister, Margot (Diane Baker), or her overly critical and stressed-out mother (Gusti Huber), we too have to dig deep in order to forgive Mrs. Van Daan her diva rants.

Even today, in an era when we're not so tightly corseted, Mrs. Van Daan reassures us that when we're under enormous strain, it's okay to let the facade slip and freak out every now and again.

WORDS TO LIVE BY

"In spite of it all, I still believe people are basically good."

MILLIE PERKINS

AS ANNE FRANK IN *THE DIARY OF ANNE FRANK*

THE KING AND I (1956)

STARS .... Deborah Kerr, Yul Brynner

DIRECTOR .... Walter Lang

WRITER .... Ernest Lehman, based on the play by Oscar Hammerstein II,
.... based on the book *Anna and the King of Siam* by Margaret Landon

ACADEMY AWARDS .... Best Actor, plus four other awards,
.... and four nominations, including Best Picture

A beautiful but willful woman, a handsome but stubborn man, a long history of stern rule by the kings of Siam, and a party involving a bunch of stuffy, wealthy Brits sounds like the ingredients for disaster, but this classic romantic musical promises that even amid the external pressures of public opinion, two opposing forces can come together, waltz divinely, and enchant audiences for years to come.

Deborah Kerr plays Anna, a Victorian-era governess and single mother who travels to Siam to teach the children of the reigning King Mongkut (Yul Brynner). She soon learns that there are so many royal heirs that even Mongkut has trouble keeping track of them. At first, Anna believes that their father only values the little urchins as testaments to his testosterone, but for all the king's gruff posturing, akimbo arms, and stiff jaw, he is actually a sweet man who adores every last one of his children, just as he cares about every last one of his subjects. When Anna suggests that the best way to maintain his tenuous hold on the country during a time of great international upheaval is to open himself to the West and Western

---

OSCAR FUN FACTS

The award for Best Screenplay (Original) in 1956 actually went to a French film that had no dialogue whatsoever—*The Red Balloon*—a charming movie about a lonely balloon that, having floated away from the boy who loved it, is joined by hundreds of colored balloons.

ways, King Mongkut invites the British for a visit, learns to dance their way, and yet maintains his integrity, dignity, and Siamese traditions. Oh, and he falls madly in love with Anna, and she with him, but because these are the 1860s by way of the 1950s, their mutual passion reaches its climax in a hoopskirt-swaying dance sequence that still sweeps us away from the pressures of our obligations. Pop this one in and let go of the need to devote every waking moment to your cause, whatever it may be.

THE AFRICAN QUEEN (1951)

STARS ....Humphrey Bogart, Katharine Hepburn

DIRECTOR ....John Huston

WRITERS ....James Agee, John Huston, based on the novel by C. S. Forester

ACADEMY AWARDS ....Best Actor, plus three other nominations

He's a gin-drinking, cigar-chomping riverboat captain badly in need of a shave, and she's a prim missionary with a high lace collar, a parasol, and a clipped Yankee accent. But stuck alone together on a thirty-foot boat in the swamps of East Africa, they find out they aren't so different after all, which just goes to show that appearances can deceive and creative casting can work out quite well from Oscar's standpoint.

After rescuing Rose Sayer (Katharine Hepburn) from the oncoming German army, Charlie Allnut (Humphrey Bogart) wends his boat downriver toward the ocean and, after a particularly harrowing encounter with white rapids, drowns his fear in a bottle of gin. Rose, however, never dreamed that a mere physical experience could be so stimulating, and it's got her primed for a daring scheme to have Charlie fashion a homemade torpedo and blow up the German steamer blocking their way at the end of the river. Together, Rose and Charlie get past their surface differences, find common ground, and, we assume, live happily ever after.

In an era of conformity, it was especially fun to watch two strong-willed characters come together. Hepburn and Bogie's performances assure us even today that true connection does not require us to give up our wonderful idiosyncrasies. Watch it when he's saying po-tay-to and you're saying po-tah-to, and take comfort in knowing that your differences don't have to be such a problem after all.

A PLACE IN THE SUN (1951)

STARS .... Montgomery Clift, Elizabeth Taylor, Shelley Winters, Herbert Heyes

DIRECTOR .... George Stevens

WRITERS .... Michael Wilson and Harry Brown,
.... based on the play *An American Tragedy* by Patrick Kearney,
.... based on the novel by Theodore Dreiser

ACADEMY AWARDS .... Best Director, Best Screenplay (Adapted),
.... plus four other awards and three nominations, including Best Picture

There are rules, you know. They're not written down anywhere, or spoken of in polite company, but in this time and place, the children of a certain comfortable class of people, such as the offspring of the factory owner Mr. Eastman (Herbert Heyes), do not dirty their elbows by rubbing them with time-card-punching employees. Eastman's nephew, George (Montgomery Clift), who has come to live with his uncle in order to lift himself up by his bootstraps, would like to follow those rules and fit in with his wealthy relatives, as it seems to be his only ticket out of poverty. Unfortunately, there is also a rule that the gorgeous, Edith Head–ballgown-clad, classically beautiful daughters of this social class—such as Angela Vickers (Elizabeth Taylor)—keep themselves pure for marriage, which puts an intense and passionate boy from the Midwest between a rock of virginity and a hard place of trying to keep quiet a sexual tryst with a factory gal who is willing to put out (Shelley Winters). Inevitably, George finds himself in the uncomfortable position of having to keep up appearances with the motorboat-party-at-the-weekend-cottage crowd while trying to placate his increasingly demanding secret squeeze. All this requires an enormous ability to lie, repress one's emotions, and concoct elaborate schemes for solving problems while acting discreet.

At a time when most of us were going to enormous lengths to conceal our complex realities, this cautionary tale about keeping secrets encouraged us to tell the truth lest we create our own American tragedy. Today it's a fascinating cautionary tale about buying into the illusion that you can lead a double life.

MISTER ROBERTS (1955)

STARS ....Henry Fonda, James Cagney, William Powell, Jack Lemmon

DIRECTORS ....John Ford and Mervyn LeRoy

WRITERS ....Frank Nugent, Joshua Logan,
.... based on the play by Thomas Heggen and Joshua Logan
.... and the novel by Thomas Heggen

ACADEMY AWARDS ....Best Supporting Actor (Jack Lemmon),
.... plus two nominations, including Best Picture

· ·

Jack Lemmon won his first of two Academy Awards (and six more nominations) for his role here as the disgruntled midshipman Ensign Pulver, who vows to confront his superior officer (James Cagney) with his anger and frustration but remains impotent.

Ensign Pulver is sick and tired of spending the Second World War on a cargo naval ship, waiting for the end of his tour of duty while Captain Morton (Cagney) makes all sorts of piddling rules that annoy the morale-challenged men. With no opportunity to become a hero, and no power to talk back to the captain, Pulver resorts to passive-aggressive stunts like setting off miniature explosions and sleeping sixteen hours a day. His immediate commanding officer, Lieutenant Roberts (Henry Fonda), dares Pulver to actually carry off one of his more outlandish pranks against the captain and admit that he did it. Meanwhile, Captain Morton doesn't even remember which one of the men is Pulver. Eventually, however, Roberts's own frustration at his inability to be a hero finally propels Pulver to recognize that you're not truly alive when you're sitting on a hotbed of repressed emotions and impulses.

WARNING LABEL

What played as boys-will-be-boys hijinks in the '50s plays much darker in this era of enlightenment about sexual harassment.

At a time when paranoia and accusations could result in grave consequences, we embraced Ensign Pulver, who encouraged us to set aside fears of retribution and speak up. See if this film doesn't inspire you to stop worrying about what people will think and voice your opinion.

GREATEST LAST LINES IN OSCAR MOVIE HISTORY

"Captain, it is I, Ensign Pulver, and I just threw your stinking palm tree overboard.
Now, what's all this crud about no movie tonight?"

JACK LEMMON
AS ENSIGN PULVER IN *MISTER ROBERTS*

AN AMERICAN IN PARIS (1951)

STARS .... Gene Kelly, Leslie Caron, Oscar Levant,
.... Nina Foch, Georges Guétary

DIRECTOR .... Vincente Minnelli

WRITER .... Alan J. Lerner

ACADEMY AWARDS .... Best Picture, Best Story and Screenplay,
.... plus four other awards and two nominations

This classic American musical features stylized courtship, stylized deception, and even stylized starvation—geez, we wish that when we're a day late and a dollar short, our white clothes stayed as pristine and our spirits as gay as Gene Kelly's do as he plays the starving painter Jerry Mulligan.

Jerseyite Jerry is pursuing his dream in Paris, following in the footsteps of the great masters, and his powerfully compact body, winning smile, and healthy color hide the fact that he hasn't a penny for a decent meal. Luckily, Jerry barely has time to confess his dilemma to his landlady as he merrily dashes out the door before he runs into a wealthy benefactress, the glamorous Milo (as in Venus de) Roberts (Nina Foch). Milo loves her boy toys and Jerry sort of plays along with her in order to get a new studio, a show, and all the oil paint a would-be Lautrec would need, but he is soon enchanted by the pixie-like Lisa (Leslie Caron). At first resistant to Jerry's charms, Lisa eventually succumbs and feels the need to toe-shoe her way across Paris with him, until, alas, she must break his heart with bad news. This, of course, causes Jerry to stop tap-dancing and start slinking about in more of a jazz style to match his mood. And lest you fear that we end on a long, low, and sorrowful Gershwin note played by a French horn, *An American in Paris* wraps up with a lover's embrace and a promise that when our lives are looking Dickensian, we must simply give in to our inner Parisian, tip our hat jauntily, and merrily dance our way to the inevitable happy ending. Who needs gritty black-and-white drama when one can be transported into the stratosphere with this exquisite confection?

THAT PARIS MAGIC

"Back home, everyone said I didn't have any talent.
They might be saying the same thing over here but it sounds better in French."

GENE KELLY

AS JERRY MULLIGAN IN *AN AMERICAN IN PARIS*

OSCAR'S RED CARPET: LOOKING GOOD, PART II

● In 1953, an actress named Sandra White showed great style when her slip fell out from under her gown as she took a tumble in the rain. Instead of panicking, she casually tossed the lingerie into her limo.

● In 1954, Best Supporting Actress nominee Katy Jurado bragged that underneath her brilliantly scarlet gown, she was wearing a red bra and panties, too.

● During the 1956 ceremony when asked what sort of fur her coat was made of, actress Anna Magnani quipped, "Italian cat." (It was, in fact, made of chinchilla fur.)

● America's sunniest and most wholesome singer, Doris Day, received indignant letters from women scolding her for wearing revealing costumes in her role as nightclub singer Ruth Etting in 1955's *Love Me or Leave Me*.

ROMAN HOLIDAY (1953)

STARS ....Audrey Hepburn, Gregory Peck, Eddie Albert

DIRECTOR ....William Wyler

WRITER ....Ian McLellan Hunter, fronting for the blacklisted, uncredited Dalton Trumbo

ACADEMY AWARDS ....Best Actress, Best Motion Picture Story, Best Costume Design,
.... plus seven nominations, including Best Picture

Princess Ann (Audrey Hepburn) is tired of keeping that smile on her face and standing in heels as she cheerfully greets hundreds of people each day when truly, she just wants to go home, curl up in bed, and sleep. Even though it looks like fun, being royalty can be an incredibly taxing responsibility. So Ann takes off her tiara, puts on a plain skirt and blouse, and sneaks out of the palace to play hooky for a while. Lucky for Ann, a kindly reporter named Joe (Gregory Peck) spots her passed out on the plaza, realizes this girl is not very street savvy, and takes her to his apartment. Even luckier for her, Joe's a nice guy who shows her the sights and keeps mum despite discovering her ruse right away. Okay, so he's planning to write an exposé for the newspaper he works for, but in the end, Joe is honorable enough to forgo selling the story of his adventure with the princess.

This classic escapist movie is a virtual deep-breathing exercise that urges us to stop pretending we're not stressed-out, face the reality that we need a break, and nurture our inner selves once in a while—without worrying so much about what other people will think.

✴ OSCAR FUN FACTS ✴

Ian McLellan Hunter, who won the award for Best Screenplay, was actually fronting for his pal, Dalton Trumbo—one of the Hollywood Ten whose screenplays won several Oscars before and after he was blacklisted. When the Academy finally recognized Trumbo posthumously in 1993 for his writing on *Roman Holiday*, they had to create another statuette to give Trumbo's widow because Hunter's son refused to give up his dad's Oscar.

ANASTASIA (1956)

STARS ....Ingrid Bergman, Yul Brynner, Helen Hayes

DIRECTOR ....Anatole Litvak

WRITERS ....Arthur Laurents, Guy Bolton,
.... based on the play by Marcelle Maurette

ACADEMY AWARDS ....Best Actress (Ingrid Bergman), plus one nomination

Is she, or isn't she, a daughter of the late Russian czar, who managed to escape the royal slaughter through miraculous means? As Anastasia, Ingrid Bergman is beautiful, mysterious, and seemingly innocent, and in an era when people were pointing fingers at imposters among us, this movie struck a chord with its message about listening to one's heart when faced with a question of trust.

"Anastasia" is suffering from amnesia and suspects she may be Anastasia Romanov, heir to the throne of Russia. A conniving Russian exile, Prince Bounine (Yul Brynner), doesn't care whether or not her memory loss and head injury are the result of having survived a brutal attack on the czar's family; he just wants a share of the dough she will inherit, so he reassures her that she's the real deal. The girl has manners, looks, and royal bearing, and can definitely pass for Russian royalty, so Bounine figures he can get the Russian Empress Dowager (Helen Hayes) to declare Anastasia the genuine article and free up all those millions just sitting there, waiting to be claimed. What he doesn't count on is the softening of his own heart, as he begins to believe that what you see is what you get, and that not everyone is as cynical and manipulative as he is.

In the Red Scare era, we all needed reassurance that sometimes, things truly were as they seemed and people really were who they professed to be. When you need a break from your own modern-day skepticism, enjoy *Anastasia*.

BORN YESTERDAY (1950)

STARS ....Judy Holliday, Broderick Crawford, William Holden

DIRECTOR ....George Cukor

WRITER ....Albert Mannheimer, based on the play by Garson Kanin

ACADEMY AWARDS ....Best Actress,
....plus four nominations, including Best Picture

· ·

Born Yesterday promises that while on the surface of American democracy there are some shady wheelings and dealings mucking things up, if you can wipe off that layer of grime, underneath you'll find that our republic is alive and breathing—and that discovery can uplift and free us all. Now, this is a pretty heady concept for a fast-paced comedy featuring the gum-cracking Judy Holliday as a Bronx babe in bleached hair and a black sequined bustier, but her ability to balance humor with a very serious message about democracy continues to win our hearts even today.

Billie Dawn (Judy Holliday) doesn't pay much attention to what's in the front of the paper, just what's at the back—you know, the funnies. But one day her thug boyfriend, Harry Brock (Broderick Crawford), hires a journalist named Paul Verrall—as in, "all truth" (*vere,* in Latin)—to teach his dame to act classy so he can do business with the congressman he plans to bribe without being embarrassed by her working-class ways (never mind Brock's crude demeanor!). Unknowingly, Brock unleashes Billie's eager mind and pure heart, and guided by Paul, she comes to discover the true meaning in those ancient documents that America was founded on. Bravely, she launches her own personal revolution and embraces her freedoms of speech, thought, and association. Considering that Holliday herself faced red charges in the McCarthy era, she must have been especially proud of her ability to bring to life a message about having faith that democracy will prevail, despite how bad things seem to be on the surface.

KEEPING IT REAL

"A world full of ignorant people is too dangerous to live in."

WILLIAM HOLDEN

AS PAUL VERRALL IN *BORN YESTERDAY*

"He always used to say, 'Never do nothing you wouldn't want
printed on the front page of the NEW YORK TIMES.'"

JUDY HOLLIDAY

AS BILLIE DAWN IN *BORN YESTERDAY*

"To all the dumb chumps and all the crazy broads,
past, present, and future, who thirst for knowledge and search for truth . . .
who fight for justice and civilize each other . . .
and make it so tough for crooks like you and me."

HOWARD ST. JOHN

AS JIM DEVERY IN *BORN YESTERDAY*

Chapter Seven

OSCAR IN THE 1940s

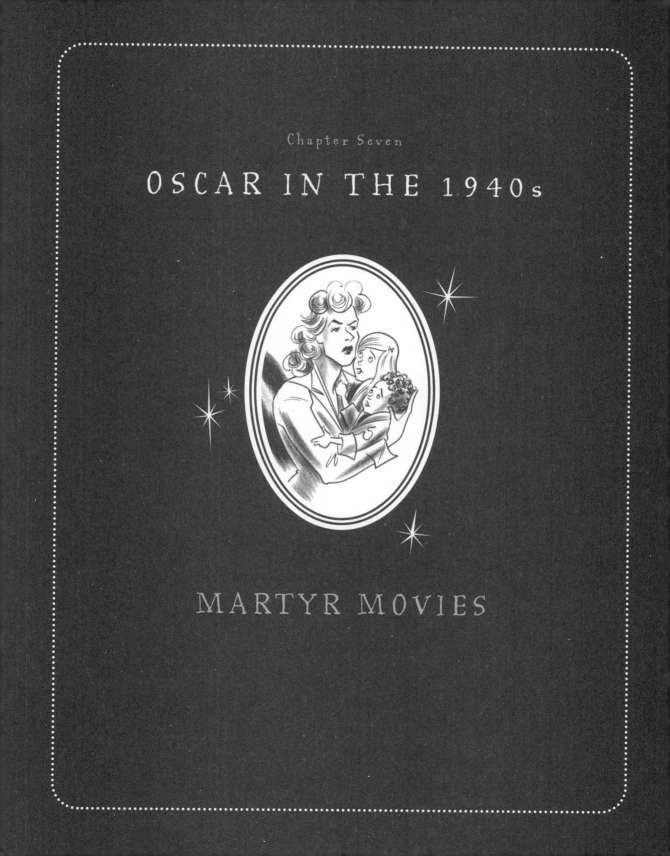

MARTYR MOVIES

Academy Awards in the '40s were, more often than not, bestowed upon movies that were designed to appeal to a generation frightened by war and uncertainty—a generation that could hide in a fallout shelter but couldn't avoid the shocks of reality pounding the ground around them, and needed lots of encouragement. Even after the war, Oscar celebrated movies featuring hardy, dignified folks who pulled themselves up by their bootstraps and reinvented their lives with nary a whimper. In these Martyr Movies, which often celebrate the soul-cleansing experience of agony, we meet fellas we can count on to keep a stiff upper lip and ladies who display corseted courage in the face of grave danger—as well as reformed divas who get their due for all those years of hedonism. These films reassure us even today that hard work, sacrifice, and taking responsibility really do matter.

THE PHILADELPHIA STORY (1940)

STARS ....Katharine Hepburn, James Stewart,
.... Cary Grant, John Howard, Virginia Weidler

DIRECTOR ....George Cukor

WRITERS ....Donald Ogden Stewart, based on the play by Philip Barry

ACADEMY AWARDS ....Best Actor (James Stewart), Best Writing (Screenplay),
....plus four nominations,
....including Best Picture and Best Actress (Katharine Hepburn)

Socialite Tracy Lord (Katharine Hepburn) is a '30s-style diva, only with more sensible clothing—although we suppose calling shoulder pads "sensible" is debatable. But while this is yet another of those strong-women-of-a-certain-era performances, it ushered in that '40s morality about self-denial and putting aside one's playfully indulgent ways, and behaving instead like a good wife and daughter.

Hepburn knew the part of Tracy Lord would restore her to her rightful place in the Hollywood heavens and put to rest forever those dreadful headlines about her being box-office poison, and she proved her critics to be myopic fools with this quintessential performance. With wicked charm, she baffles, annoys, and—of course—wins the heart of not one, not two, but three men: her ex-husband (Cary Grant), her fiancé (John Howard), and a cynical newspaper reporter (James Stewart) who comes to realize that Tracy is no empty-headed, shallow rich girl but a force of nature to be reckoned with. Indeed, they all talk about

✦ WARNING LABEL ✦

Though it's considered a classic movie ha-ha moment, that scene where Cary Grant shoves Kate Hepburn might make you want to snap a few golf clubs yourself (*grrr!*).

Tracy as if she were some sort of goddess. Well, at the very least, she's the patron saint of independent women who haven't the time or inclination to coddle weak men who ought to be solving their own damn problems. After all, she's got a horse to ride, a wedding to plan, one-liners to zing, a diva-in-training kid sister to tease, and a thick mane of red hair to be tossed back as she enjoys a cigarette out on the veranda.

But as befits the constrained mood of the era, *The Philadelphia Story* morphs into a morality tale about how a mature woman ought to stand by her man at all costs, forgive her unrepentant philandering papa, and quit thinking about herself so much. Ugh. We prefer to crunch popcorn over the pedantic dialogue about shoulds and oughts, and simply enjoy Kate in her I-can't-be-bothered-with-your-nonsense, wisecracking prime.

DIVA DIAMONDS

C. K. Dexter Haven (Cary Grant): Sometimes, for your own sake, Red, I think you should've stuck to me longer.
Tracy Lord (Katharine Hepburn): I thought it was for life, but the nice judge gave me a full pardon.
FROM *THE PHILADELPHIA STORY*

"Oh, we're going to talk about me again, are we? Goody."
KATHARINE HEPBURN
AS TRACY LORD IN *THE PHILADELPHIA STORY*

A SIMPLE THANK-YOU WOULD SUFFICE

"If I didn't think you meant so well, I'd feel like slapping your face."

. . . .

"I'm a spoiled child, an imbecile to be humored. Maggie the Martyr. You make me sick."
MARY ASTOR
AS SANDRA KOVAK IN *THE GREAT LIE*

THE GREAT LIE (1941)

STARS .... Bette Davis, Mary Astor, George Brent

DIRECTOR .... Edmund Goulding

WRITER .... Lenore J. Coffee,
.... based on the novel by Polan Banks

ACADEMY AWARDS .... Best Supporting Actress (Mary Astor)

· ·

When Oscar voting took place post–Pearl Harbor, we were newly sobered and looking for uplifting stories of sacrifice, but reluctant to let go of that self-absorbed diva behavior that's so deliciously shocking. Mary Astor scored big with the Academy with her portrayal of a New York society woman who drinks too much, smokes too much, and slaps the help around. But she meets her match in Bette Davis, who despite her soft do, big eyes, and prim frocks, isn't about to give up on her good man (George Brent) just because he got drunk and was seduced by Sandra (Mary Astor), a shameless New York musician with a bad attitude and a long cigarette holder. When Maggie (Bette Davis) learns that her rival is expecting the pitter-patter of tiny feet, her nurturing instincts are roused, and she bribes Sandra into letting her be a selfless and devoted mom, freeing Sandra to be a self-centered career gal. Thus, in one of the silver screen's most melodramatic plot twists, Maggie ends up in a remote Arizona cabin during a windstorm caring for the pregnant Sandra, who launches into a foul-tempered rant about having to eat her vegetables and skip cocktail hour.

This extraordinarily dysfunctional on-screen relationship and its happily-ever-after denouement reassured us all that powerful though those rich-bitch society types may be, they'll be sorry in the end, and it's us good girls with hearts of gold and backbones of steel, who are willing to stand by our men, who triumph. Today it's a wonderfully campy indulgence sure to help you beat the martyr blues.

THE LOST WEEKEND (1945)

STARS . . . . Ray Milland, Jane Wyman, Phillip Terry

DIRECTOR . . . . Billy Wilder

WRITERS . . . . Billy Wilder, Charles Brackett, based on the novel by Charles Brackett

ACADEMY AWARDS . . . . Best Picture, Best Director,
. . . . Best Actor, and Best Writing (Screenplay),
. . . . plus three nominations

. . . .

Don (Ray Milland), a novelist suffering writer's block over his sophomore effort, has been nipping at the bottle too much of late to pay attention to all the hoopla about a group called Alcoholics Anonymous that has been opening chapters throughout the country. At the urging of his well-meaning fiancée, Helen (Jane Wyman), Don's doing his best to believe that all he needs to get on the wagon of sobriety is a nice long weekend in the country with trees, grass, cold well water, and fresh apple cider. Actually, the only thing he can think about is that bottle of rye hanging on a string outside his window—the one he'll be yanking up as soon as Helen's footsteps fade down the hallway. Don's brother, Wick (Phillip Terry), is less than convinced of Don's new sobriety and is suspicious when his brother comes up with an excuse to catch the late train out of the city, but he doesn't know how to prevent the potential disaster of an unsupervised Don spending the weekend in an alcoholic haze. So, before you know it, that spooky theremin is playing, fake-looking spiders are crawling the walls, and poor Don is begging the local bartender to take pity on him with just one shot, dammit, just one.

Luckily, Don has good old Helen to look out for him. Helen's a woman who will humiliate herself by making the rounds of neighborhood bars asking after him, sleeping on his doorstep, and standing by her man even as he vows that all he needs to clean himself up is her love and a book contract for his sure-to-be-best-selling memoir (yeah, right).

We shudder to think what sort of crazy notions moviegoers of 1945 walked out of the theater with regarding suitable treatments for alcohol dependency. And with the book *Codependent No More* a few decades off, it's difficult to watch Helen feeling empowered by a love she thinks is unconditional but that we know is hopelessly codependent and worthy of its own 12-step support group. But in the end, this is a compelling cautionary tale about what happens when a man who has terrific potential gets a bit too loose, doesn't take care of business, and falls into the abyss.

GREAT LAST LINES
IN OSCAR MOVIE HISTORY

"I know, Belinda. You don't have to say anything."

LEW AYRES
AS DR. RICHARDSON IN *JOHNNY BELINDA*

"I'm not brave. It isn't like that at all.
When the time comes, when it comes, I will do my best."

BETTE DAVIS
AS SARAH MULLER IN *WATCH ON THE RHINE*

MILDRED PIERCE (1945)

STARS .... Joan Crawford, Jack Carson, Zachary Scott, Eve Arden, Ann Blyth

DIRECTOR .... Michael Curtiz

WRITERS .... Ranald MacDougall, William Faulkner, Catherine Turney, ... based on the novel by James M. Cain

ACADEMY AWARDS .... Best Actress (Joan Crawford), ... plus five nominations, including Best Picture

No film has captured the martyr syndrome quite like *Mildred Pierce* starring Joan Crawford as Mildred, who caters a first-class guilt feast as this legendary doormat mom turned fast-food queen who is victimized by her spoiled, selfish, thoughtless, ungrateful, and thoroughly heartless daughter, Veda (Ann Blyth). Veda is probably the worst child ever portrayed on-screen, without a single redeeming quality to her credit. The girl is content to enjoy the privileges of her mother's hard labor while looking down on her as a common waitress. And what's worse, she's constantly complaining about her mother's downscale decorating and bad fashion sense.

Add a faithless husband, the untimely death of her good daughter, and a bum murder rap to Mildred's heavy load, and you've got a masochistic mom cocktail that must have made everybody in the '40s, not to mention today, feel so much better by comparison.

OSCAR FUN FACTS

Joan Crawford was so uncomfortable with the thought of attending the Academy Awards ceremony and having to look gracious if she didn't win Best Actress for *Mildred Pierce* that she feigned the flu . . . but greeted reporters on her doorstep shortly after the announcement that she had won, wearing a lovely brown negligee and a perfectly made-up face.

SHARPER THAN A SERPENT'S TOOTH

"With this money, I can get away from you.
From your chickens and your pies and your kitchens and everything
that smells of grease. I can get away from this shack with its cheap furniture.
And this town with its dollar days, its women who wear uniforms,
and its men who wear overalls."

ANN BLYTH

AS VEDA IN *MILDRED PIERCE*

HAMLET (1948)

STARS .... Laurence Olivier, Jean Simmons, Eileen Herlie, Norman Wooland

DIRECTOR .... Laurence Olivier

WRITER .... William Shakespeare (tweaked by Laurence Olivier)

ACADEMY AWARDS ..... Best Picture, Best Actor (Laurence Olivier), plus two other awards
.... and three nominations

This was the first in a series of adaptations of Shakespeare's plays that Laurence Olivier wrote, produced, and directed in this era. These were a real hit, perhaps because we were all infatuated with Winston Churchill specifically, and Britain's Dunkirk spirit in general, but also because Olivier's Shakespearean cinema allowed us to linger for a moment in a higher world, before life took us all downtown to the school of hard knocks.

Hamlet, the Prince of Denmark, had particular appeal in the up-on-the-cross '40s, because he is one of the biggest drama queens in dramatic history. And to sweeten the pot even more, he is very hung up on his mother. In fact, in some Shakespearean circles, Olivier's portrayal is still referred to by the Shakespeare set as the "Oedipal Hamlet." Olivier's performance in the central role is one long pout by a mama's boy who wants to do the right thing and avenge his father's murder, but somewhere along the way he lost all his mojo, and not even his father's perturbed spirit can resurrect it. And then, of course, there's that pesky attraction to his trampy mother, who had the unmitigated gall to bury her husband and then marry his brother before the "funeral baked meats" had even cooled to room temperature. And at the end, of course, because this is one of the greatest martyr-syndrome plays ever written, the stage is littered with bodies—and Academy Awards.

BING CROSBY,
THE GOOD FATHER O'MALLEY

Crooner Bing Crosby did a lot of hokey road pictures with Bob Hope, but he is also remembered for his classic portrayal of the friendly neighborhood priest in *Going My Way* and its sequel, *The Bells of St. Mary's*. Despite the fact that in real life, Papa Bing was, by all reports, not exactly warm and cuddly to his sons, and conveniently ignored their existence years later when he did those happy family Christmas specials with cherry-cheeked family number 2, Bing was as snuggly a paternalistic figure on-screen as they come, always willing to put himself out for the good of those under his fatherly wing. These are great movies to watch when you're feeling put-upon and in need of a little paternal nurturing, Cinematherapy-style, because Father O'Malley is a daddy who can always be counted on to provide a few chuckles, a melodic tune or two, and, of course, miracles on demand.

GOING MY WAY (1944)

STARS ....Bing Crosby, Barry Fitzgerald

DIRECTOR ....Leo McCarey

WRITERS ....Frank Butler, Frank Cavett,
.... based on a story by Leo McCarey

ACADEMY AWARDS ....Best Picture, Best Actor (Bing Crosby),
.... Best Supporting Actor (Barry Fitzgerald),
.... and Best Director, plus three more awards and three nominations

Having forgone worldly passions in order to serve God and the community, the gentle Father O'Malley (Bing Crosby) humbly submits to the bishop's new orders to become the curate at a New York City church facing bank foreclosure. Rather than break the heart of Father Fitzgibbon (Barry Fitzgerald), the elderly priest he'll be replacing, Father O'Malley submits quietly to the old curate's demanding and even arrogant ways and keeps secret the fact that he is in charge. No, the good-ly young priest just tips his straw hat, breaks into song whenever possible, and goes along with whatever his "boss" says. Ever patient with the local gang of scruffy boys, he persuades them to give up petty crime for afternoons spent crooning "Silent Night," "Ave Maria," and, if they're lucky, a cheeky number like "Would You Like to Swing on a Star." As for the crotchety old priest, what can the good young father do but smile indulgently and serenade him to sleep with "Tura Lura Lura"? And when tragedy comes to the church, Father O'Malley uplifts the spirits of all those in his charge, unites opposing forces, and saves the day. This one's the perfect tonic for when things aren't going your way and you wish some nice daddy figure would drop in from the heavens and quietly solve all your problems.

THE BELLS OF ST. MARY'S (1945)

STARS .... Bing Crosby, Ingrid Bergman, Henry Travers

DIRECTOR .... Leo McCarey

WRITER .... Dudley Nichols, based on a story by Leo McCarey

ACADEMY AWARDS .... Best Sound Design, plus seven nominations, ... including Best Picture

The sequel to *Going My Way*, which was being filmed even as its predecessor was scooping up statues on Oscar night, was no disappointment to those who wanted a reprise of Father O'Malley's paternalistic generosity with a tiny hint of mischievous behavior (although in the end, Oscar was less wowed by the sequel and nearly shut it out). This time around, however, it isn't Father O'Malley who—whoops!—shatters a window with a line drive he's hit while bonding with the kiddies. Nope, it's kindly Sister Benedict (Ingrid Bergman) re-enacting that very scene, and trying to outdo Father O'Malley in the anything-for-the-parish department.

When you need a miraculous cure for the no-one-cares-about-my-problems blues, *The Bells of St. Mary's* is as soothing as warm milk before bed—and potentially as soporific if you can't giggle a bit at its retro wholesomeness.

GASLIGHT (1944)

STARS .... Ingrid Bergman, Charles Boyer

DIRECTOR .... George Cukor

WRITERS .... John Van Druten, Walter Reisch, John L. Balderston,
.... based on the play *Angel Street* by Patrick Hamilton

ACADEMY AWARDS .... Best Actress (Ingrid Bergman), plus one other award
.... and five nominations, including Best Picture

· ·

Ingrid Bergman, whose wide-eyed terror is unforgettable in this suspense thriller, struck a chord with the Academy. After all, in the '40s, we loved to be reminded that nice girls had better watch out for men who would exploit them—and that there would always be a chivalrous gentleman to rescue us.

Young, beautiful, and trusting Paula Alquist (Ingrid Bergman) falls for a suave and seemingly wealthy man (Charles Boyer), marries him, and starts to wonder why the gaslights in her home are beginning to flicker—while the servants and her husband deny it. And that's not all: stuff is missing from her purse. Pictures disappear from her walls. There are strange noises coming from the attic. And her husband keeps going on about how she's merely nervous and distraught and really, she shouldn't even think about the fact that her mother lost her mind and had to be institutionalized because, of course, it can't be genetic. It takes a good friend and a willingness to believe in her own perceptions to pull Paula from the brink of danger. Watch this when you're tired of being told you're paranoid and be assured that good instincts never lie.

REBECCA (1940)

STARS .... Joan Fontaine, Laurence Olivier,
.... Judith Anderson, Florence Bates

DIRECTOR .... Alfred Hitchcock

WRITERS .... Joan Harrison, Michael Hogan,
.... Philip MacDonald, Robert E. Sherwood,
.... based on the novel by Daphne du Maurier

ACADEMY AWARDS .... Best Picture, Best Cinematography,
.... plus nine nominations

Wishing you could be whisked away by a loving older man who sets you up financially, renders irrelevant your lack of career or personal direction, and gives you your own English country mansion to rattle about in? This movie is a great reminder that abdicating responsibility for your life decisions and letting some guy steer the boat is never a wise idea, even if it does make you feel cozy on a cold autumn morning.

Our shy heroine (Joan Fontaine) is thrilled when wealthy Maxim DeWinter (Laurence Olivier) deigns to marry down and rescues her from a life as a paid companion to a most dis-

---

NANCY'S MOMENTOUS MINUTIAE: METHOD DIRECTING

Since Laurence Olivier wanted his girlfriend, Vivien Leigh, to play Fontaine's part in *Rebecca*, he was not exactly warm to Joan Fontaine on set. Director Alfred Hitchcock realized that this was stirring up in Fontaine feelings of shyness, awkwardness, and inadequacy, all of which were appropriate for her on-screen, schoolgirlish character, so he decided to tell Fontaine that everyone on the set—not just Olivier—couldn't stand her. The result was an Academy Award–nominated performance and, we're sure, major stress and paranoia.

agreeable old biddy (Florence Bates). However, for all Maxim's patronizing promises to care for his new bride, and his silly little flirtatious remarks about how she ought never to grow up, our gal is going to have to face reality. Frankly, her new knight in shining armor has something buried deep in the darkest waters of his soul that is going to surface one day and demand to be dealt with. And until the new Mrs. DeWinter stops with the apologetic bowing and scraping before the servants and starts getting some of that upper-class entitlement, she's going to be haunted by the late Rebecca DeWinter's reputation as the hostess with the mostess, as well as by Rebecca's favorite freakishly devoted maid, Mrs. Danvers (Judith Anderson). Honey, we know you hate confrontation, but here's a good rule of thumb: When the hired help starts fingering the carefully preserved lingerie of its late owner and suggesting that you focus on your inadequacies and lean a little further out that third-floor French window, it is time to put down your foot and speak up.

When you're feeling the need to go below deck and let someone else take over, get it out of your system with this cautionary tale about avoiding responsibility, and be happy you won't have to deal with the coroner's inquest the morning after.

JOHNNY BELINDA (1948)

STARS .... Jane Wyman, Lew Ayres, Charles Bickford, Agnes Moorhead

DIRECTOR .... Jean Negulesco

WRITERS .... Allen Vincent, Irmgard von Cube,
.... based on the play by Elmer Harris

ACADEMY AWARDS .... Best Actress (Jane Wyman),
.... plus eleven nominations, including Best Picture

. . . .

Is there any more vulnerable gal on the silver screen than Belinda McDonald (Jane Wyman), a deaf and mute young woman who has never gone to school and doesn't know life outside of the farm where she helps her parents bake pies and carry hay? With her wide eyes and sweet smile, Belinda is a walking target for exploitation. Lucky for her, she's got a friend in Dr. Richardson (Lew Ayres), a small-town doctor willing to risk his reputation to stand by Belinda when she is suddenly discovered to be pregnant and the community wants her head on a plate—and the doctor's too, since they assume he was doing more than merely teaching her sign language on his long visits to the McDonald farm.

Wyman's portrayal of a disabled woman who is courageous despite having been taken advantage of and having been condemned by the very people who should be protecting her, tugged at the heartstrings of audiences who wanted to believe that they too could find the strength to bear their burdens. Today it plays kind of hokey, but it's the perfect no-one-understands-or-appreciates-me movie for a Sunday afternoon.

OOPS! DID I SAY THAT OUT LOUD?

"I won this award by keeping my mouth shut and I think I'll do it again."

JANE WYMAN

UPON ACCEPTING THE AWARD FOR BEST ACTRESS
FOR HER ROLE IN *JOHNNY BELINDA*

SUSPICION (1941)

STARS .... Joan Fontaine, Cary Grant

DIRECTOR .... Alfred Hitchcock

WRITERS .... Samson Raphaelson, Joan Harrison, Alma Reville,
.... based on the novel *Before the Fact* by Anthony Berkeley

ACADEMY AWARDS .... Best Actress (Joan Fontaine),
.... plus two nominations, including Best Picture

....

In this woman-in-jeopardy cautionary tale about being too trusting and letting yourself be taken advantage of, Joan Fontaine plays Lina, good girl in a very bad situation. She falls hard for a charming playboy (Cary Grant), marries him, and then finds herself choking back her anger, smoothing the lines on her face, and asking him politely how his job search is going and why her favorite family heirlooms are sitting in a pawnbroker's window. Again and again, Lina tries to make excuses for her bad boy, telling others that he's simply a bit child-like and naïve, and with a little patience and discipline from her, he'll straighten out. However, she neglects to notice that she's in a Hitchcock movie, and her only hope of escape is if the studio pressures Hitch to slap on a last-minute, it's-gonna-be-okay scene to soften the dark ending the director had envisioned.

This is a fun movie to watch when a certain someone has been dishonest and manipulative with you, and you need to laugh about your overly trusting nature.

THE FARMER'S DAUGHTER (1947)

STARS ....Loretta Young, Joseph Cotten, Ethel Barrymore, Charles Bickford

DIRECTOR ....H. C. Potter

WRITERS ....Allen Rivkin, Laura Kerr, based on the play by Hella Wuolijoki

ACADEMY AWARDS ....Best Actress (Loretta Young),
....plus one nomination for Best Supporting Actor (Charles Bickford)

Here's a movie about truth, justice, and the American way that takes an earnestly disapproving attitude toward all those ancient, off-color farmer's-daughter-and-the-salesman jokes.

When a sleazy local salesman tricks a simple Swedish-American farm girl named Katrina (Loretta Young) into an act that compromises her reputation among small-town folk, she writes off her plans to attend nursing school—because surely everybody has heard about her shame. Rather than embarrass her hardworking and decent family back home, even though she's done absolutely nothing wrong, Katrina hides out as a domestic servant. What a gal, thinking only of her family!

As a maid in the house of a wealthy congressman named Glen Morley (Joseph Cotten), "Katie" charms him with her down-to-earth political opinions and, of course, her ability to brew an exceptionally good cup of coffee, which for many a decade was a crucial résumé point for any gal looking to get ahead. Before you can say "Olaf's been at the aquavit again," Katie's career options have expanded once more. Yes, it looks like she has a good shot at

OSCAR FUN FACTS

During World War II, the golden Oscar statue was made out of plaster because metal was so scarce.

being the local Carol Mosely Braun, only wearing braid buns at her ears and speaking in a singsong accent, ja.

Alas, Katie's past comes to haunt her, and the now-smitten Morley is unable to protect the woman he loves from his snobby mother, who wants Katie to crawl back to the farm and hide under a rock. Will Katie crumble under the pressure of having that dreadful incident from her past smeared all over the papers? Or is she of sturdy farmer stock, the kind of gal who recognizes that speaking up for oneself and yet knowing how to whip up a mean batch of glogg come Christmastime are equally important skills?

The Farmer's Daughter gives nod to such notions as honesty, integrity, and duty while insisting that in America, a plainspoken woman with a hefty dose of common sense is a national resource not to be squandered. Watch it when you need a boost of confidence in your own ability to rise above a smear campaign, ja.

GENTLEMAN'S AGREEMENT (1947)

STARS ....Gregory Peck, Dorothy McGuire, Celeste Holm, Anne Revere

DIRECTOR..Elia Kazan

WRITER........Moss Hart, based on an article in *Cosmopolitan* magazine and the book by Laura Z. Hobson

ACADEMY AWARDS ....Best Picture, Best Director,
....Best Supporting Actress (Celeste Holm), plus five nominations

In *Gentleman's Agreement*, Gregory Peck is the kind of guy we all like to think we'd be if faced with a challenge requiring self-sacrifice: He sticks to his principles and perseveres even when he meets with social disapproval. And most astonishingly, he makes Dorothy McGuire, normally an avatar of the good wife, look like an uppity bitch, which has got to be a silver-screen first.

To be fair, Kathy Lacey (Dorothy McGuire) isn't particularly mean or self-absorbed, but when her boyfriend, journalist Philip Green (Gregory Peck), takes on the assignment of writing about anti-Semitism, the ugly little prejudice underneath Kathy's surface peeks out. But can we blame her for asking him to stop posing as a Jew amongst the reigning WASPs of New England long enough for her to have a lovely engagement party complete with cocktails, cordial chatter, and a houseful of wealthy guests puffed up to poster size thanks to their false sense of entitlement? Look, when you're registered at Tiffany's and you've got all the suburban Connecticut socialites attending your nuptials, a gal can't be blamed for not wanting to ruffle any feathers by exposing hypocrisy and prejudice, just for the damn weekend.

But of course, Philip, being the kind of man he is, insists on keeping his non-Jewish identity under wraps until his series of articles appears. The man is determined to shed light on the bigotry that is woven into the fabric of polite society. Can Kathy let go of her own need for a place in the social register and a spectacular collection of housewares, in the service of a good cause? Or will her selfishness cause Philip to succumb to the charms of a woman (Celeste Holm) ready to stand by a man who does the right thing, no matter what the cost?

When you're feeling unsupported in your efforts to make the world a better place, *Gentleman's Agreement* will encourage you to believe that your own bravery and willingness to tolerate discomfort will help others to let go of their own fears.

HOW GREEN WAS MY VALLEY (1941)

STARS..Roddy McDowall, Sara Allgood,
....Donald Crisp, Walter Pidgeon, Maureen O'Hara

DIRECTOR..John Ford

WRITER...Philip Dunne,
....based on the novel by Richard Llewellyn

ACADEMY AWARDS ....Best Picture, Best Director,
....Best Supporting Actor (Donald Crisp),
....plus two other awards and five nominations

When times are hard, and frugality and sacrifice are the order of the day, people often turn to movies that celebrate the simple joys of life while smoothing over the rough edges of memory better than Vaseline on a camera lens. This one's the kind of film that's all warm and fuzzy on the surface, but if you squint a little, you'll see some very harsh edges.

The story of Huw (Roddy McDowall), the youngest son in a family of Welsh coal miners at the turn of the twentieth century, *How Green Was My Valley* is a picture postcard in black and white, featuring rolling hills, harmonious voices raised in song, a bonny, bonny lass (Maureen O'Hara, who else?), an inspiring young preacher (Walter Pidgeon), a proud papa (Donald Crisp), and a strong and brave mama (Sara Allgood) at the heart of everything.

As cheap labor in the countryside increases, the Morgan family—Mom, Dad, daughter, and a houseful of brothers—are rocked by dissention over whether to unionize. Meanwhile, the sorrows pile up: Serious illness befalls young Huw and his mother; Huw's older sister (Maureen O'Hara) becomes infatuated with an unattainable man; and, of course, there's a horrendous mining accident or two to remind them to cherish every moment in that lush, green valley while they can.

In the mood to forget your troubles, practice the art of selective memory, and enjoy an idealized version of the past? If you're willing to overlook some of the more disturbing realities of life among folks whose choices aren't exactly as wide-open as the daffodil-strewn fields, *How Green Was My Valley* will feel like a big cashmere blanket around your shoulders.

YANKEE DOODLE DANDY (1942)

STARS .... James Cagney, Joan Leslie, Walter Huston

DIRECTOR .... Michael Curtiz

WRITERS .... Robert Buckner, Edmund Joseph

ACADEMY AWARDS .... Best Actor (James Cagney), plus two other awards
.... and five nominations, including Best Picture

· ·

The pyrotechnic James Cagney won his first Academy Award for his performance as George M. Cohan in this wartime biopic about a flag-waving showman who reminds us that while war is hard, vaudeville is harder, and that come what may, the show must go on.

The story begins with a drenched George M. Cohan bounding up the steps of the White House to meet President Roosevelt, who starts to reminisce about the famous Cohans of Boston. We then flash back to the very beginning of Cohan's career in the theater, built on such national favorites as "Over There," "You're a Grand Old Flag," and "The Yankee Doodle Boy," supported by lots of patriotic production numbers and Cagney tap-dancing to beat the band, even though he had no dance training whatsoever. Midpoint in his career, Cohan is called out by the critics for his fluffy flag-waving, and he parries with a serious play, which, of course, bombs. Cohan returns to producing and starring in the nationalistic pep rallies that made him famous, and winds up receiving the Medal of Honor, and reminding us, years before JFK, to ask not what our country can do for us, but what we can do for our country.

During World War II, Home Front Movies kept morale high and helped ease the anxiety of movie watchers who feared the worst fates for their loved ones overseas while they struggled at home to make do. Interestingly, none of these popular Home Front Movies, which Oscar gave nod to, shied away from portraying the harshness of war in a world turned upside down. Okay, so they got a little gooey and sticky-sweet at times, but they reassure us that whatever happens, if we can stick together and have faith, we'll always land on our feet.

MRS. MINIVER (1942)

STARS .... Greer Garson, Walter Pidgeon, Teresa Wright, Richard Ney

DIRECTOR .... William Wyler

WRITERS .... George Froeschel, James Hilton,
.... Claudine West, Arthur Wimperis,
.... based on the novel by Jan Struther

ACADEMY AWARDS .... Best Picture,
.... Best Actress (Greer Garson),
.... Best Supporting Actress (Teresa Wright),
.... Best Writing (Screenplay),
.... Best Director, Best Cinematography,
.... plus six other nominations

Winston Churchill was in love with this movie, and FDR was so impressed by the vicar's rousing speech at the end that he had it printed up on leaflets that were dropped over occupied France. Truly, the classic scene in the backyard fallout shelter where a British mother (Greer Garson) and father (Walter Pidgeon) softly read bedtime stories to their rosy-cheeked children while German bombs whistle and shake the ground, makes you want to dry your eyes, belt out "God Save the Queen," and vigorously wave the Union Jack. Unfortunately, the journey to those more stirring moments takes the scenic route through wholesome domestic folderol involving a nice young lady (Teresa Wright) and a nice young soldier (Richard Ney), and flower-show preparations so dull that you're actually grateful that a Nazi finally shows up to inject some drama into the proceedings.

In the end, the rousing messages here about carrying on despite horrific losses, discovering the importance of community, and standing together against fear shine through brightly. *Mrs. Miniver* is a fascinating nugget from a more wholesome era when we desperately needed our own everyday courage reflected on-screen.

✦ THE HUMAN COMEDY (1943) ✦

STARS .... Mickey Rooney, Fay Bainter, Van Johnson, Donna Reed

DIRECTOR .... Clarence Brown

WRITER .... Howard Estabrook,
.... based on the novel by William Saroyan

ACADEMY AWARDS .... Best Writing (Original Motion Picture Story),
.... plus four nominations, including Best Picture

Once again, a lovable teenage actor provides the spunk and sparkle in a Home Front picture about regular folks, while his female family members (Fay Bainter and Donna Reed) form a warm blanket of love around him. Homer Macauley (Mickey Rooney) is on the hyper side, getting into tussles at school and such, but he's as responsible as they come. With money tight in the household, Homer gets a job as a telegram messenger to help out, even as he keeps up his grades, treats his freckle-faced kid brother, Ulysses (Jackie "Butch" Jenkins), with nothing but affection, and does all his chores without complaint. But just as things are getting a tad too treacly, the death telegrams start coming in, and with a brother overseas, Homer prays that he won't have to deliver one of those dreaded "Regret to inform you" missives to his own household.

A real tearjerker, *The Human Comedy* may be shameless in its sentimentality, but when you're in the mood for some retro sweetness, you'll appreciate this tribute to the power of love and the importance of opening our doors and our hearts to others.

THE BEST YEARS OF OUR LIVES (1946)

STARS .... Fredric March, Myrna Loy, Teresa Wright, Michael Hall, ... Dana Andrews, Virginia Mayo, Harold Russell, Cathy O'Donnell

DIRECTOR .... William Wyler

WRITER .... Robert E. Sherwood, ... based on the novel *Glory for Me* by MacKinlay Kantor

ACADEMY AWARDS .... Best Picture, Best Actor (Fredric March), ... Best Supporting Actor (Harold Russell), Best Writing (Screenplay), ... Best Director, plus two other awards, one nomination for Best Sound, ... and an honorary Academy Award to Harold Russell for "bringing hope .... and courage to his fellow veterans through his appearance .... in *The Best Years of Our Lives*"

Shortly after the war ended, when patriotic fervor was running high, *The Best Years of Our Lives* won the hearts of Academy voters with its story of three soldiers and the families they returned to. It reminded us that after the upheaval of a war, it's not so easy to hang up the old uniform and get back to business as usual, so we had better do right by those returning vets who gave their all for us.

Al Stephenson (Fredric March), an officer, is chagrined to discover that his wife (Myrna Loy), his daughter, Peggy (Teresa Wright), and his son, Rob

(Michael Hall), have grown quite used to his absence, so that he feels a bit like a war trophy stuck in an easy chair as they go about their lives around him. Fred Derry (Dana Andrews) returns to the bride he impetuously married before shipping off (Virginia Mayo) and discovers he made a mistake in rushing to the altar—and to complicate matters, he is falling in love with Al's daughter, Peggy. And sweet-natured Homer Parrish (Harold Russell) returns home to his fiancée, Wilma (Cathy O'Donnell), without his arms or his optimism—can the two of them carry on and become man and wife now?

Despite some annoying and unfair digs at pacifists and Rosie the Riveters, this movie does a fine, honest job of portraying "what happens next," and offers a glimpse of what it is like for soldiers and their families to adjust to a peacetime reality that presents its own challenges.

✳ SINCE YOU WENT AWAY (1944) ✳

STARS ....Claudette Colbert, Jennifer Jones,
....Shirley Temple, Monty Woolley

DIRECTOR ....John Cromwell

WRITER ....David O. Selznick,
....based on the novel *Together* by Margaret Buell Wilder

ACADEMY AWARDS ....Best Musical Score,
....plus eight other nominations, including Best Picture

In this Home Front classic, a teenage Shirley Temple supplies the perkiness while Claudette Colbert, playing her mom, supplies the stoicism. Good mother Anne Hilton (Colbert) sends her husband off to war and realizes the best way to financially support her two daughters (Shirley Temple and Jennifer Jones) is to rent out a room in their comfy suburban home. The boarder, Colonel Smollett (Monty Woolley), is as peppery as can be, wanting his eggs cooked just so and stubbornly refusing to bond with this trio of ladies. Indeed, he's so grumpy that he lets his grandson go off to war without making peace with the lad. This, of course, is the perfect setup for a lesson in love and loss, getting past petty differences, and creating and relying upon community support in hard times. With its honest depictions of men who came home from the war missing vital parts of themselves, *Since You Went Away* does its best to resist oversentimentality.

LAUNDERING THE SOUL

"Air raids, indeed. Those wretched Germans! They wouldn't dare!"

DAME MAY WHITTY

AS LADY BELDON IN *MRS. MINIVER*

"This is not only a war of soldiers in uniform,
it is a war of the people—of all the people—and it must be fought
not only on the battlefield but in the cities and in the villages,
in the factories and on the farms, in the home,
and in the heart of every man, woman and child who loves freedom."

HENRY WILCOXON

AS THE VICAR IN *MRS. MINIVER*

CASABLANCA (1942)

STARS .... Humphrey Bogart, Ingrid Bergman,
.... Paul Henreid, Claude Rains,
.... Sidney Greenstreet, Peter Lorre, Dooley Wilson

DIRECTOR .... Michael Curtiz

WRITERS .... Julius J. Epstein, Philip G. Epstein, Howard Koch,
.... based on the play *Everybody Comes to Rick's* by Murray Burnett and Joan Alison

ACADEMY AWARDS .... Best Picture, Best Director,
.... Best Writing (Screenplay), plus five nominations

· ·

This classic tale of two lovers who martyred themselves for a greater cause is one of the most famous love stories in Hollywood history, not only because it was an opportunity for wartime movie audiences to warm themselves by the fire of patriotic heroism, but because it combined the cynicism of a war-torn society with the hope that even in the midst of an emotional desert, love and self-sacrifice can and will endure.

Humphrey Bogart stars as Rick Blaine, a world-weary and cynical expatriate who has given up on true love and idealism, choosing instead to live out the remainder of his days as the owner of a gin joint in Casablanca where Germans, French, Americans, and Italians join together to drown their sorrows and turn a dishonest buck. Then one day, out of the blue, Ilsa (Ingrid Bergman), who is a well-coiffed metaphor for Rick's lost innocence, walks into his gin joint and reawakens Rick's heroic heart.

Unfortunately, in this era of martyrdom, which placed self-sacrifice above all other things, where even a happy ending to a timeless love story doesn't escape the obligations of history, Rick's restored nobility must immediately sacrifice itself for a greater cause.

Casablanca comforts us with the message that it is better to give than to receive, and that the problems of three people, even in a war-torn world, really do amount to a hill of beans.

CLASSIC MARTYR MOMENTS

"I have already given him the best, knowing he is German and would take it anyway."

S. Z. SAKALL

AS CARL IN *CASABLANCA*

"You know, Rick, I have many a friend in Casablanca, but somehow,
just because you despise me, you are the only one I trust."

PETER LORRE

AS UGARTE IN *CASABLANCA*

"Where I'm going, you can't follow.
What I've got to do, you can't be any part of.
Ilsa, I'm no good at being noble,
but it doesn't take much to see
that the problems of three little people don't amount to
a hill of beans in this crazy world. Someday you'll understand that.
Now, now … Here's looking at you kid."

HUMPHREY BOGART

AS RICK IN *CASABLANCA*

WATCH ON THE RHINE (1943)

STARS .... Bette Davis, Paul Lukas, George Coulouris, Eric Roberts

DIRECTORS .... Herman Shumlin, Hal Mohr

WRITERS .... Dashiell Hammett, Lillian Hellman,
.... based on the play by Lillian Hellman

ACADEMY AWARDS .... Best Actor (Paul Lukas),
.... plus three nominations, including Best Picture

Though she made her mark in the early '30s as a diva, by the war years Bette Davis, along with many of her fellow actresses, was dutifully playing the martyr on-screen. Gone were the furs and the platinum dye jobs: In *Watch on the Rhine*, she's a girdle-wearing mom with a controlled brunette coif. And gone were the snappy one-liners and the insouciance: The wartime Miss D. was too busy wringing her hands, feeling guilty about her own needs, and delivering stirring speeches about devotion to the cause of freedom to give in to self-pampering.

Of course, it's always amusing to see Bette Davis launch into one of her crescendos of agony, and here she's got plenty of fodder for overwrought Max Steiner compositions featuring plenty of wailing violins. Sarah (Bette Davis) is an American woman with a German husband, Kurt Muller (Paul Lukas), whom she follows, Ruth-like, wherever he goeth, living on bread crusts, sharing cramped quarters with mice, and propping up the spirits of her three stoic children as they move throughout Europe, trying to escape the clutches of the fascists. Kurt, you see, is a member of the Underground, and thus Sarah will face any deprivation or danger to support him in his noble work. She doesn't even allow herself a drink, let alone romantic reminiscences in cheap gin joints in Casablanca. Nope, Sarah is content to beam proudly at her husband as well as her precocious youngest son (Eric Roberts), who has to be the most cloying brat in movie history. Sarah intends to live up to the heroic example of her late father, a distinguished judge, and do what she must for the cause of justice. So when a sleazy Romanian gambler (George Coulouris) threatens Kurt's safety, Sarah's big eyes fill with tears as she confronts the fact that her husband must walk into the storm and face almost certain death. And should he fall, well, just give her the briefest of moments to indulge in self-pity and then she'll dab at her eyes and gladly send her son off to take his father's place. Now, how's that for a stirring sentiment worthy of the self-sacrificing '40s?

A SMALL PRICE TO PAY

"We are not here to show that we are brave,
and not to be modest either and say,
'I am not important. Let me take the risk.'
He takes the risk who is entitled to it."

PAUL LUKAS

AS KURT MULLER IN *WATCH ON THE RHINE*

"Papa said the only men on earth worth their time on earth
are the men who would fight for other men.
Papa said, we have struggled through from darkness
but man moves forward with each day and each hour to a better, freer life.
That desire to go forward, that willingness to fight for it,
cannot be put in a man, but when it is there . . ."

BETTE DAVIS

AS SARAH MULLER IN *WATCH ON THE RHINE*

OSCAR IN THE 1930s

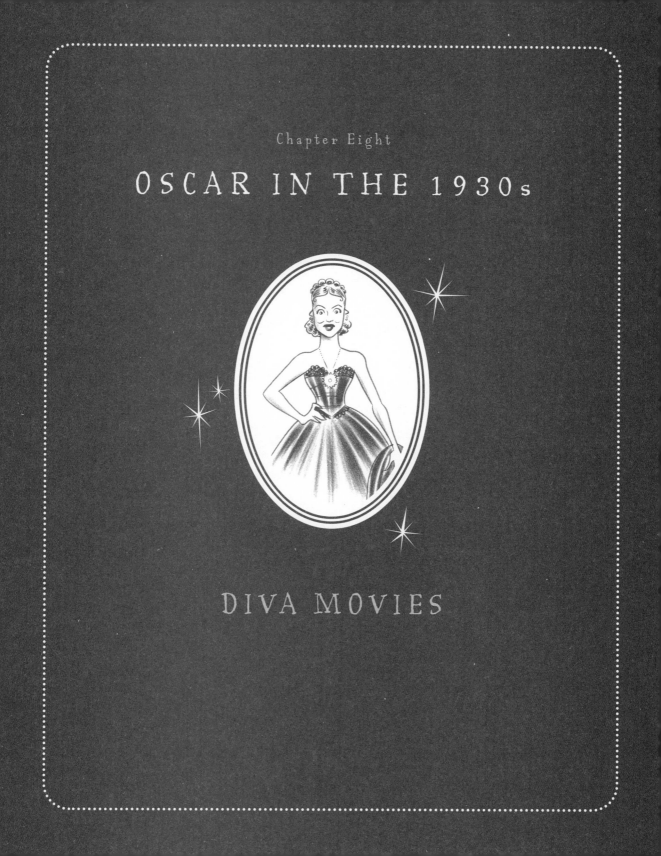

DIVA MOVIES

During the Great Depression we were all eager for a vicarious thrill and an escape into someone else's far more glamorous problems. It's no surprise that in this era, many Academy Awards were bestowed upon movies featuring jewel-and-fur-draped divas whose tribulations included everything from a fashion faux pas that results in disaster to a legendary jinx that drives a gal to floozy behavior in gin joints. We even wanted their men to be over-the-top, from self-indulgent rich boys to financially reckless, womanizing showmen. Whether these divas learned a lesson at the end of the last reel or not, Oscar in the 1930s embraced a range of self-indulgent yet basically good characters who reminded us that we all deserve pampering sometimes. These Diva Movies are some of the greatest cinematic medicine ever made, perfect for indulging in after a long, hard day of behaving oneself.

JEZEBEL (1938)

STARS ....Bette Davis, Henry Fonda,
.... George Brent, Margaret Lindsay, Fay Bainter

DIRECTOR ....William Wyler

WRITERS ....Clements Ripley, Abem Finkel,
.... John Huston, Robert Buckner,
.... based on the play by Owen Davis Sr.

ACADEMY AWARDS ....Best Actress (Bette Davis),
.... Best Supporting Actress (Fay Bainter),
.... plus three nominations, including Best Picture

This is another one of those classic Bette Davis bad-girl performances that women of the '30s ate up and we ought to immerse ourselves in far more often. Coquettish, manipulative, and outrageously selfish behavior might not play in the real world, but for a couple of hours at least, one can vicariously enjoy the wicked, wicked ways of a thoroughly unrepentent jezebel.

In this pre–Civil War drama, an eyelash-batting southern belle, who doesn't care a fig about her reputation, browbeats her southern gentleman fiancé, Preston "Pres" Dillard (Henry Fonda), into catering to her every whim. But when Miss Julie (Bette Davis) takes it a step too far and dares to wear a red silk dress to a white-dress ball, her shameless hussy ways so infuriate the straight-laced Pres that he drops her like the red-hot vixen she is. Alas, Miss Julie must now enter her blue period, given to sighing spells and dark brooding, fretted over by her aunt (Fay Bainter). But, of course, when Pres returns, demure Yankee gal (Margaret Lindsay) by his side, Miss Julie rises to the occasion. She pulls out every south-

WARNING LABEL

The happy-singing-slaves scenes are best gotten through with a little eyeball rolling and julep drinking.

ern-belle trick she has hidden behind those big shining eyes, determined to smack some sense into Pres once and for all, and make him realize that she is, indeed, a goddess.

We're sorry to say that, once again, we moviegoers have our fun spoiled with one of those "don't try this at home, ladies" plot twists that punishes Miss Julie for being too self-involved. But at least we are allowed a wildly histrionic Bette Davis speech and violin-crescendo ending that honors the drama queen inside all of us. So when you're feeling unappreciated and in need of some self-nurturing, pour yourself a mint julep, don that red silk negligee, and pamper yourself with *Jezebel*.

BETTE BITES

"This is 1852, dumplin', 1852, not the dark ages.
Girls don't have to simper around in white just because they're not married."

BETTE DAVIS
AS JULIE MARSDEN IN *JEZEBEL*

JULIE (BETTE DAVIS): For heaven's sakes, don't be gentle with me now.
Do you think I wanna be wept over?
I've gotta think, to plan, to fight.
AUNT BELLE (FAY BAINTER): But you can't fight marriage!
JULIE: Marriage, is it! To that washed-out little Yankee?
Pres is mine! He's always been mine.
And if I can't have him . . .
FROM *JEZEBEL*

IT HAPPENED ONE NIGHT (1934)

STARS..Clark Gable, Claudette Colbert

DIRECTOR..Frank Capra

WRITER..Robert Riskin,
.......................based on the *Cosmopolitan* magazine article "Night Bus" by Samuel Hopkins Adams

ACADEMY AWARDS..Best Picture, Best Actor (Clark Gable),
....Best Actress (Claudette Colbert),
....Best Director, Best Writing (Adaptation)

The best way to tone down a diva's spoiled-brat behavior and create a self-assured creature who doesn't drive you crazy with ridiculous demands is to match her up with a diva-esque fella and let them fall in love and bring out the best in each other.

That's exactly what happens in this story of an overindulged, fabulously wealthy heiress named Ellie Andrews (Claudette Colbert) and a too-cocky-for-his-own-good newspaper reporter named Peter Warne (Clark Gable). Ellie has impetuously married a wealthy noble of some unnamed European country in order to spite her controlling father, and when Pop announces he's put through for an annulment, she dives off his yacht and runs away to the nearest bus station. Quickly relieved of her wallet and belongings—Ellie is not exactly street-smart—she is forced to hook up with a sarcastic, unemployed journalist who desperately needs to sell his "Guess who I met on the bus" story to get his job back. After all, Peter can provide her with chivalrous male protection, wise budgeting advice, and an egg-and-doughnut breakfast when needed.

OSCAR FUN FACTS

It Happened One Night was the first movie to sweep Best Picture, Best Actor, Best Actress, and Best Director, a feat not duplicated again until 1975, with *One Flew Over the Cuckoo's Nest.*

Ellie and Peter miss no chances to take each other down a peg—they butt heads over everything from who's the better hitchhiker to who's the true master of doughnut dunking. Yet their romp through the backwoods and bus depots of Lower Horsetail is so filled with sexual chemistry that it's only a matter of time before he stops with the male posturing and she gives up this King Whatshisname nonsense and they get a room already—and a marriage license, of course, having maintained their chastity by draping a blanket over a rope as a room divider in all the cheap motels they've stayed in.

This flick's a great reminder that there are advantages to that diva-esque sense of entitlement, including the ability to land on one's feet despite limited resources, a chance for netting a fellow traveler along life's journey who shares your sense of adventure and fun, and the opportunity to make a lasting silver-screen impression as you dash across a field to embrace life wholeheartedly.

OSCAR'S RED CARPET:
DIVA IN THE HOUSE

- Claudette Colbert didn't want to be in *It Happened One Night* because she was approached with the job offer right before she was about to leave on vacation. To pay Miss Colbert her very high salary without going broke, producer Hal Cohn told director Frank Capra to make the movie in four weeks, and indeed, Colbert started shooting forty-eight hours after first being approached with the role (the lack of budget and time is reflected in the very limited number of sets and costumes). According to Frank Capra Jr., Miss Colbert complained every day, told her friends afterward that it was the worst picture she had ever made, and showed up reluctantly at the Academy Awards in street clothing, ready to catch a train out of town. When she won, the rather surprised Claudette Colbert said simply, "Thank you," but then, thinking better of it, ran back to the podium for a quick "I owe this to Frank Capra" before departing.

- In 1934, Bette Davis was none too happy that Claudette Colbert beat her out for Best Actress but it could have been worse: Shirley Temple, at the height of her career, was deserving of a Best Actress Oscar herself, and what's more, the six-year-old knew it. However, feeling that a win by the curly-haired tyke would result in diva-esque hissy fits on the part of every adult actress in town, the powers that be in the Academy voted to give Miss Temple a "special" juvenile Oscar. Gracious as Miss Temple was at the time, years later she wrote in her autobiography how she felt ripped off, a victim of other actresses' jealousy.

- Bette Davis was one of the few actresses to show up to the Academy Awards ceremonies in 1935, because the Academy was supporting the studio system against actors seeking greater contract freedom. Miss D. was not about to miss her chance to accept a statue for Best Actress, and that she did. The very next day, she began a labor strike against the studio.

- Wallace Beery was considered for the role of Captain Bligh in *Mutiny on the Bounty* but didn't want to play opposite Clark Gable because he couldn't stand him. Meanwhile, James Cagney was in the neighborhood when the movie was being filmed off Catalina, California, and asked if he could join in the fun as an extra, which the director agreed to.

DANGEROUS (1935)

STARS	Bette Davis, Franchot Tone, Margaret Lindsay
DIRECTOR	Alfred E. Green
WRITER	Laird Doyle
ACADEMY AWARDS	Best Actress (Bette Davis)

When Miss D. was passed over for an Academy Award for her appearance as a vain, self-centered, downright bitchy prostitute in 1934's *Of Human Bondage*, it seemed only fair to reward her with the golden statue for her 1935 performance as a vain, self-centered, downright bitchy actress in *Dangerous*. And believe us, no one, but no one, does diva bitch better than Bette Davis.

Joyce Health (Bette Davis) is a walking cautionary tale about what the fates have in store for a vitally tempestuous creature who soars like a comet into the starry skies of celebrity: She smashes to earth, causing a wave of mass destruction. The awesome power of Joyce's jinx is so legendary that they whisper of it still: how her leading man was killed on opening night, how marriages crumbled around her and producers fell to financial ruin, and how people jumped off balconies in her wake. Yes, this star shone so brilliantly that she scorched the earth behind her and now has been reduced to sucking down cheap gin in a sleazy bar among the shooting galleries, slurring the speeches of Juliet in a dramatic display before falling flat on her fanny in a drunken stupor.

Of course, Joyce does down-and-out has-been with such power and charisma that she can't help but be rescued by a wealthy architect named Don (Franchot Tone). Don, it seems, has been smitten with her ever since as a youth he watched her perform and felt compelled to dash off to Paris to pursue the artistic life. Now, however, he's merely a working joe with a society gal fiancée (Margaret Lindsay) and a lovely cottage in the Hamptons where he chivalrously takes Joyce to dry out.

Joyce, however, proves to be a regular wildcat, spewing insults at Don and smashing his liquor cabinet so she can pour herself another stiff one. Yet, over time, thanks to the healing power of Don's love, she begins to mellow out and starts to believe in herself again. But will her bad luck destroy her opportunity to shine on the stage once more, as well as her chance for true love with a man who appreciates her?

Sadly, this is one of those flicks that takes the easy road in the final reel and presents us with a chastened and domesticated diva who repents of her ambitions and thirst for glamour and the spotlight. Until it takes that last wrong turn, however, *Dangerous* allows us a vicarious, thrilling, roller-coaster ride through the life of a drama queen who fearlessly lives life to its fullest.

BETTE BITES

"Pity? Pity? You dare feel sorry for me? You, with your fat little soul
and your smug face, picking your way so cautiously through a pestile existence.
Why, I've lived more in a day than you'll ever dare live. Pity for me?
That's very funny, because I've never had any for men like you."

BETTE DAVIS

AS JOYCE HEATH IN *DANGEROUS*

"You cad! You dirty swine! I never cared for you, not once!
I was always makin' a fool of ya! Ya bored me stiff—I hated ya!
It made me sick when I had to let ya kiss me.
I only did it because ya begged me, ya hounded me and drove me crazy!
And after ya kissed me, I always used to wipe my mouth!
Wipe my mouth!"

BETTE DAVIS

AS MILDRED ROGERS IN *OF HUMAN BONDAGE*

MUTINY ON THE BOUNTY (1935)

STARS .... Charles Laughton, Clark Gable, Franchot Tone, Movita

DIRECTOR .... Frank Lloyd

WRITERS .... Talbot Jennings, Jules Furthman, Carey Wilson,
.... based on the novel by Charles Nordhoff and James Norman Hall

ACADEMY AWARDS ... Best Picture, plus seven nominations, including three for Best Actor

It's a big-screen battle of the divas in this maritime epic, which won Best Picture in 1935 and was the highest-grossing film of the year. It was also the most expensive movie productions ever. Well, it costs a lot of money to maintain two world-class divas on a floating metaphor for the ultimate victory of humanity over cruelty, breeding over brawn, and compassion over fear—not to mention how much money it must have taken to talk Clark Gable into wearing those ridiculous trousers.

Charles Laughton stars as cruel diva Captain Bligh, who rules his ship with an iron fist and seems to take an unwholesome pleasure in watching his underlings suffer for no apparent reason. Since, according to maritime law, the captain is the undisputed master of his domain while out at sea, no matter how out of hand Bligh gets in his demands, no one can question him on pain of death. No one, that is, until Fletcher Christian (Clark Gable) not only leads the men to mutiny and sends his rival diva packing, but even manages to snag a few Tahitian teenagers on the side. And in the end, while Mr. Christian's shiny gold buttons were a little tarnished as a consequence of his brand of vigilante justice, he nevertheless became a beacon for Depression-era audiences and all of us today who need reassurance that tolerance and mercy, in the end, will always triumph over cruelty.

DIVAS ON DECK

"I've never known a better seaman, but as a man, he's a snake.

He doesn't punish for discipline.

He likes to see men crawl.

Sometimes, I'd like to push his poison down his own throat."

· · · · · · · · · · · · · · · ·

"These men don't ask for comfort. They don't ask for safety . . .

They ask only the freedom that England expects for every man.

If one man among you believed that—one man!—

he could command the fleets of England. He could sweep

the seas for England if he called his men to their duty, not by flaying

their backs but by lifting their hearts—their . . .That's all."

CLARK GABLE

AS FLETCHER CHRISTIAN IN *MUTINY ON THE BOUNTY*

"They respect but one law—the law of fear . . .

I expect you to carry out whatever orders I give, whenever I give them."

· · · · · · · · · · · · · · · ·

"Casting me adrift thirty-five hundred miles from a port of call!

You're sending me to my doom, eh?

Well, you're wrong, Christian!

I'll take this boat, as she floats, to England if I must.

I'll live to see you—all of ya—

hanging from the highest yard arm in the British fleet!"

CHARLES LAUGHTON

AS CAPTAIN BLIGH IN *MUTINY ON THE BOUNTY*

CAPTAINS COURAGEOUS (1937)

STARS .... Spencer Tracy, Freddie Bartholomew, Melvyn Douglas

DIRECTOR .... Victor Fleming

WRITERS .... Mark Connelly, John Lee Mahin, Dale Van Every,
.... based on the novel by Rudyard Kipling

ACADEMY AWARDS .... Best Actor (Spencer Tracy),
.... plus three nominations, including Best Picture

In the '30s, we may have loved to watch a conceited diva flouncing about in farcical situations, but for a drama to be morally palatable, we needed to see her—or him—taught a lesson in humility.

In this flick, our diva is Harvey (Freddie Bartholomew), a deliciously insufferable boarding-school brat. His father's servants despise him so much that they refer to the child as "it," and his pop, the tycoon (Melvyn Douglas), calls him a junior Machiavelli. Harvey has a habit of tossing his brown forelock and sneering at everyone around him, and is not above sucking down five ice cream sodas in a row to prove the awesome extent of his gluttony in the consumerist world that he's destined to rule someday. But alas, Harvey will have to grow up and become an honorable and honest businessman if he is to take his place in society and inherit his father's business empire without contributing to moral decay on Wall Street, which many felt was to blame for the dire financial circumstances in our country. Yep, Harvey's carrying a lot of weight on those English flannel-covered shoulders.

Good old Fate steps in, however, to provide a convenient storm at sea that rocks the ship Harvey is sailing on, sending him into the drink. The sputtering boy is rescued by a fisherman, Manuel (Spencer Tracy), who has a zest for his trade, a love for song, a rather dubious Portuguese accent, and a Mike Brady–esque perm to match his Mike Brady–esque speeches about life and love. Onboard the fishing schooner where Manuel is employed, Harvey gets a good dose of soul-cleansing manual labor. It's all very humbling for Harvey, and soon he's washing cod livers and baiting hooks with the best of them, refusing to wince when one pierces his hand. But of course, the plot simply has to twist back to him taking up the mantle of noblesse oblige.

A manly sort of morality tale, *Captains Courageous* cautions us against taking the diva act too far, lest we wind up with a spectacularly maudlin ending, stock market instability, and cuticles covered in fish guts.

MANUEL'S MANLY WISDOM

"Say, that's the best kind of songs–when you feel good inside.
Like trade winds, she just come out."

"Say, sometimes a song so big and sweet inside, I, just can't get him out.
And then I look up at the stars and maybe cry, it feels so good.
Don't you never feel like this?"

SPENCER TRACY

AS MANUEL IN *CAPTAINS COURAGEOUS*

THE GREAT ZIEGFELD (1936)

STARS ....William Powell, Myrna Loy, Luise Rainer

DIRECTOR ....Robert Z. Leonard

WRITER ....William Anthony McGuire

ACADEMY AWARDS ....Best Picture, Best Actress (Luise Rainer),
....Best Dance Direction, plus four nominations

Clocking in at three hours, this movie is a diva in itself, with its long-winded story line, its parade of cameos, and its lavish re-creation of the extravagant costumes and sets of the Ziegfeld follies—a perfect tribute to Florenz Ziegfeld (William Powell), an over-the-top showman who made an art of excessive consumption.

Ziegfeld had humble-enough beginnings as a carnival barker, but as befits a celebrated American icon, he pulled himself up by borrowed bootstraps and inherent chutzpah to become a great Broadway producer. Always the gambler, he was ambitious and confident whether he was rich or poor.

Shortly after his first success with a strongman act, Ziegfeld uses his considerable charm and lots of orchids to woo a flighty French singer named Anna Held (Luise Rainer) away from her manager. He makes Anna a star, marries her, dallies a bit too often with the showgirls, gets

NANCY'S MOMENTOUS MINUTIAE: STOP THE SET— I WANT TO GET OFF

In *The Great Ziegfeld*, the Oscar-winning dance sequence for "A Pretty Girl Is Like a Melody" consists of a single, continuous shot and is populated by almost 200 smiling gals and guys in hoopskirts and tails, many of whom rotate on a giant spiraling platform that looks like a black-and-white birthday cake. This scene alone cost almost a quarter of a million dollars to film.

dumped, marries the talented and lovely Billie Burke (Myrna Loy), has a family, falls on hard times, makes a comeback, and loses it all in the Crash. As the movie ends, he stares off into the distance above the camera lens, excitedly imagining his next show as the chorus swells, the dancing girls are superimposed, and his voice trails off. Cue the angelic voices.

When you too could use a little of that can-do attitude, the promise of recovery from tough times, and a stunning display of glitz, glamour, lamé, and tap-dancing, pop in *The Great Ziegfeld* and dream, dream, dream.

WHAT WERE THEY THINKING?
THE AWFUL TRUTH (1937)

STARS .... Cary Grant, Irene Dunne, Ralph Bellamy

DIRECTOR .... Leo McCarey

WRITERS .... Sidney Buchman, Viña Delmar,
.... based on the play by Arthur Richman

ACADEMY AWARDS .... Best Director,
.... plus five nominations, including Best Picture

The Awful Truth was one of the definitive screwball comedies of its era and its genre starring Cary Grant and Irene Dunne, a scintillating duo of divas who kept America giggling through most of a difficult decade.

Married couple Jerry (Cary Grant) and Lucy (Irene Dunne) flirt with a "continental" lifestyle and immediately suspect each other of cheating. And despite all of their pretense at modern broad-minded thinking, they immediately file for a divorce. The only trouble is, they have to wait sixty days for the divorce to become final. While they wait for this interim period to elapse, Jerry and Lucy try to out-diva each other, vamping and camping their way into moviegoers' hearts and establishing a whole new genre of battle-of-the-sexes movies that is still with us to this day. In the end even the permissive and continental attitudes of this adapted

'30s Broadway stage sensation can't keep Jerry and Lucy apart, and they fall back into each other's arms, content to hang up their diva crowns in order to hold on to each other, which must have been a comforting message to a Depression-era audience that needed to remember that be it ever so humble, there's no place like home. While *The Awful Truth* did take Best Director, it lost out for Best Picture to *The Life of Emile Zola*, which has long since disappeared from the video shelves, while *The Awful Truth* has remained a favorite staple for all of us conflicted divas who need to remember that home is where the heart is—particularly if home includes Cary Grant (age 33), who, unbelievably, was not even nominated for this performance. What were they thinking?

HE SAID, SHE SAID

"I wish Lucy would go out and get some fun for herself now and again. It would do her good. That's the trouble with most marriages today. People are always imagining things. The road to Reno is paved with suspicions. And the first thing you know, they all end up in a divorce court."

CARY GRANT
AS JERRY IN *THE AWFUL TRUTH*

"I wouldn't go on living with you if you were dipped in platinum. So go on, divorce me. Go on, divorce me! It'll be a pleasure."

IRENE DUNNE
AS LUCY IN *THE AWFUL TRUTH*

SHE DONE HIM WRONG (1933)

STARS ....Mae West, Cary Grant, Noah Beery

DIRECTOR ....Lowell Sherman

WRITERS ....Harvey F. Thew and John Bright,

.... based on the play *Diamond Lil* by Mae West

ACADEMY AWARDS ....None.
....One nomination for Best Picture

There's never been a diva quite like Mae West, the original Material Girl, who shocked and titillated '30s audiences with her love of diamonds and double entendres, and never apologized for anything. In this screen adaptation of her bawdy stage play *Diamond Lil*, Mae and her costar, Cary Grant, ricochet like pinballs through a vaudevillian-style plotline that is virtually incomprehensible, and largely auxiliary anyway next to the inimitable Miss West, who winked and leered and quipped her way into Oscar history without ever winning an Oscar.

Mae plays Lady Lou, a naughty but nice femme fatale who likes diamonds better than men, and men better than morality, and who gave us a badly needed breath of fresh air and a walk on the wild side at a time when many had closed the windows and thrown the dead bolts to keep the wolf from the door. *She Done Him Wrong* was a box-office smash for Columbia, but it lost out for Best Picture to *Cavalcade*, which has long since disappeared from public view, while Mae West shines on.

MAE'S MALLOWS

"I wasn't always rich.
No, there was a time when I didn't know where
my next husband was coming from."

....

"Listen, when women go wrong, men go right after them."

....

"Why don't you come up some time and see me?"

MAE WEST

AS LADY LOU IN *SHE DONE HIM WRONG*

MY MAN GODFREY (1936)

STARS .... Carole Lombard, William Powell,
.... Gail Patrick, Alice Brady, Mischa Auer

DIRECTOR .... Gregory La Cava

WRITERS .... Morrie Ryskind, Eric Hatch,
.... based on the novel by Eric Hatch

ACADEMY AWARDS .... None.
.... Nominated for six awards, including
.... Best Actor (William Powell),
.... Best Actress (Carole Lombard),
.... Best Supporting Actor (Mischa Auer),
.... Best Supporting Actress (Alice Brady),
.... Best Director, and Best Writing (Screenplay)

Throughout the years Oscar has favored extravaganzas for Best Picture, but often those films fade into obscurity while smaller films stand the test of time. *My Man Godfrey*, which was well nominated but completely shut out by the Academy, is a classic screwball comedy, which mostly takes place in one wealthy family's very low-budget drawing room, and includes lots of jokes about action offscreen, which we imagine did a lot to keep the props and scenery budget in check. And yet the comic performances, the razor-sharp dialogue, and the sheer brilliance of its idiocy make it one of the most beloved movies of the black-and-white era.

As the movie opens, socialite Irene Bullock (Carole Lombard) is engaged in a scavenger hunt with the rubies-and-sable-wrap crowd. On the lookout for a man who is down on his luck—which is on her list of items to find, somewhere after "a billy goat"—she checks out the local garbage dump and discovers Godfrey (William Powell). Since he's nice enough to play along, and she's ditzy enough to get away with this callous frivolity at the expense of a homeless man, Godfrey ends up working as her family's butler, nursing their inevitable hangovers, feeding them one-liners, and generally acting as a comic foil for them before he and Irene fall madly in love. We can't even begin to imagine what sort of marriage this odd couple will have, but this wickedly funny farce still has the fizz of a fine champagne seventy-odd years after the cork was popped.

PASS THE BOX OF BON MOTS

"All you need to start an asylum is an empty room
and the right kind of people."

EUGENE PALLETTE
AS ALEXANDER BULLOCK IN *MY MAN GODFREY*

"If you're going to be rude to my daughter,
you might as well at least take your hat off!"

ALICE BRADY
AS ANGELICA BULLOCK IN *MY MAN GODFREY*

Irene (Carole Lombard): Can you butle?
Godfrey (William Powell): Butle?
Irene: Yes, we're fresh out of butlers.
The one we had left this morning.
FROM *MY MAN GODFREY*

GONE WITH THE WIND (1939)

STARS ....Vivien Leigh, Clark Gable,
....Olivia DeHavilland, Leslie Howard, Hattie McDaniel

DIRECTOR...Victor Fleming

WRITER ....Sidney Howard,
....based on the novel by Margaret Mitchell

ACADEMY AWARDS ....Best Picture, Best Director,
..........................Best Writing (Screenplay), Best Actress (Vivien Leigh),
...............................Best Supporting Actress (Hattie McDaniel),
....plus four other awards and five nominations

In this Depression-era epic, audiences got their money's worth with the crème de la crème of visual feasts, but more than that, we got a sweeping story that elevated the tale of one southern belle to a metaphor for personal triumph over the misfortune of world upheaval. This, of course, was food for the soul when food for the belly was scarce thanks to a collapsed world economy.

When the movie opens, Scarlett O'Hara (Vivien Leigh) is a full-fledged diva who won't settle for the affections of one man, or even two. No, Miss Scarlett feels entitled to have every man in three counties salivating at her feet, and every woman in sight pea green with envy. Bitchy, disloyal, and self-absorbed? Yes. But how can you not love a woman who, at the age of 16, can discombobulate the power elite of the entire population of Atlanta and its out-lying counties with her flirtations and clever machinations?

When beau Ashley Wilkes (Leslie Howard) thwarts Scarlett's nuptial plans by marry-ing his milquetoast cousin, Melanie (Olivia DeHavilland), Scarlett impetuously weds

WARNING LABEL

As with *Jezebel*, pour yourself a stiff mint julep and prepare for some cringe-worthy stereotypes of happy-go-lucky slaves.

Melanie's mush-mouthed brother out of spite and secretly awaits her chance to steal Ashley away. It doesn't come for many years, though, and in the meantime Scarlett suffers hunger, deprivation, fear, the loss of her beloved mother, and near homelessness. After many years of crawling out of poverty and amassing wealth, Scarlett finally gets her chance to nail Ashley. And yet suddenly she becomes aware of the real riches she's acquired: not her buckets of money and overly opulent lifestyle, but a man who loves her through and through (Clark Gable as Rhett Butler), an absurdly loyal best friend in Melanie, and an indomitable spirit—

OSCAR'S RED CARPET: THE BELLE OF THE BALL, 1939

Gone with the Wind is a movie that's not only about a diva, it is a diva. Filmed in brilliant Technicolor while most of its competitors were in black and white, clocking in at barely under four hours instead of the standard two, scored with majesty by the melodramatic Max Steiner, and featuring a cast and crew of thousands, producer David O. Selznick's epic *Gone with the Wind* confidently swept the Academy Awards of 1939, leaving in its dust such underawarded classics as *Stagecoach*, *The Wizard of Oz*, *Wuthering Heights*, *Mr. Smith Goes to Washington*, and *Of Mice and Men*. Yes, *Gone with the Wind* was the belle of the ball. Academy Awards presenter Bob Hope even joked that it was nice of everyone to come out that evening just to honor David O. Selznick.

While two of the movie's actresses (Vivien Leigh and Hattie McDaniel) won Oscars for acting, Best Actor nominee Clark Gable lost to Robert Donat for his role as a kindly Latin teacher in the forgettable *Goodbye, Mr. Chips*. Perhaps it was karma, for Gable had pulled a diva act and lobbied to get "women's director" George Cukor replaced with his favorite director, Victor Fleming, a real man's man who Gable knew would infuse a little testosterone into the play and prevent Leigh from upstaging him with her performance. Fleming got the job and went on to win the Best Director award, but the joke was on Gable: After Cukor was canned, Vivien Leigh secretly snuck out to Cukor's house for advice on how to play her scenes, and consequently won the Best Actress award. Moral of the story: Never, ever try to outmaneuver Miss Scarlett.

all of which make Ashley look like a rather pale prize. It's at this point that Scarlett puts the immature and coldhearted behavior of her youth behind her and embraces a more mature sense of entitlement.

So, will she win back Rhett's affections? Perhaps, perhaps not, but the lesson of *Gone with the Wind* is that sometimes, taking a diva-esque view of matters and being cognizant of one's own power, even to the point of being overly optimistic, is necessary if one is to achieve happiness.

MISS SCARLETT'S DIVA DIAMONDS

"War, war, war!
This war talk's spoiling all the fun at every party this spring.
I get so bored I could scream!
Besides, there isn't going to be any war."

. . . .

"Marriage, fun? Fiddle-dee-dee! Fun for men, you mean."

. . . .

"Great balls of fire! DON'T bother me anymore,
and DON'T call me sugar!"

. . . .

"As God is my witness,
as God is my witness they're not going to lick me!
I'm going to live through this and when it's all over,
I'll never be hungry again! No, nor any of my folk.
If I have to lie, steal, cheat, or kill!
As God is my witness, I'll never be hungry again!"

VIVIEN LEIGH
AS SCARLETT O'HARA IN *GONE WITH THE WIND*

LET ME KISS YOU, KATE

An icon of American womanhood, Katharine Hepburn burst onto the screen way back in 1932 and nabbed her first Oscar the next year in her third movie appearance, setting the stage for more than seven decades of enchanting audiences. She was a movie star with endless wit, style, determination, humor, and brilliance, with a New Englander's penchant for speaking her mind in a way that was as bracing as a stiff wind over a frosty lake. At a time when pants on women still drew audible gasps, the trousered Kate confidently strode into the modern era demanding her due, breaking the rules, refusing to suffer fools, and encouraging the rest of us to follow suit. Oscar noticed, too: She garnered twelve nominations in her lifetime, and took home four statues—more wins than any other actress, before or since.

LITTLE WOMEN (1933)

STARS ....Katharine Hepburn, Joan Bennett, ...Douglass Montgomery, Spring Byington

DIRECTOR ....George Cukor

WRITERS ....Sarah Y. Mason, Victor Heerman, ...based on the novel by Louisa May Alcott

ACADEMY AWARDS ....Best Writing (Adaptation), ...plus two nominations for ....Best Picture and Best Director

The Academy overlooked Katharine Hepburn's classic performance in this flick, wowed by her role in *Morning Glory* later that year, but it's Hepburn's vivacious turn as the tomboyish Jo March in *Little Women* that we modern American women can't seem to get enough of. Maybe we're mesmerized by the way she runs through the woods and bounds over fences despite the layers of pantalets and crinolines she wears as the hoopskirted Jo, who refuses to walk like a lady because she's so filled with exuberance. Maybe we're taken in by the way she giggles nervously, then tosses her head back with pride, and later sobs into her pillow because she's

CHAPTER EIGHT: OSCAR IN THE 1930s: *DIVA MOVIES*

bravely cut off her beautiful long hair to raise money to help her family. Or maybe it's that despite the ridiculous bonnet and girlie getup she's been forced into, Jo is as independent and forthright as a gal can be, with plans for a career and an unwillingness to marry the first nice eligible bachelor who falls at her knees (Douglass Montgomery). Yep, Jo is penning her own story, and by Christopher Columbus, she'll make us believe that we can do it, too.

MORNING GLORY (1933)

STARS .... Katharine Hepburn, Douglas Fairbanks Jr., Adolphe Menjou

DIRECTOR .... Lowell Sherman

WRITER .... Howard J. Green,
.... based on the play by Zoe Akins

ACADEMY AWARDS .... Best Actress (Katharine Hepburn)

Kate plays a young actress hungry for a career on the New York stage, so much so that she has devoted enormous amounts of time, energy, and money to learning how to walk and talk—and apparently, she's also taken several master classes in diva demeanor. Prattling on in a vainglorious manner about her love of the theater, living on nothing but hope and coffee, Eva insists she will be a great actress. Oh, all right, we admit that she thoroughly embarrasses herself at a big-time producer's cocktail party with her champagne-soaked recital of Hamlet's soliloquy and Juliet's balcony speech. And yes, when she finally gets onstage, she stinks up the joint with her lousy acting. But despite her outrageous diva-esque behavior, it's clear that this morning glory will defy the odds, show them all, and bloom for a long, long time to come.

STAGE DOOR (1937)

STARS .... Katharine Hepburn, Ginger Rogers,
.... Adolphe Menjou, Andrea Leeds, Lucille Ball,
.... Eve Arden, Ann Miller, Gail Patrick

DIRECTOR .... Gregory La Cava

WRITERS .... Morrie Ryskind, Anthony Veiller,
.... based on the play by Edna Ferber and George S. Kaufman

ACADEMY AWARDS .... Nominated for
.... Best Supporting Actress (Andrea Leeds),
.... Best Picture, and two other awards

In another would-be-starlet-with-a-narcissistic-streak role, Kate manages to make
what ought to seem like a very obnoxious character into a role model for believing
in oneself and embracing one's destiny. But flanked by several wisecracking co-
divas (Ginger Rogers, Eve Arden, et al.), Hepburn once again inspires us to believe
that a little chutzpah will go a long way toward helping us achieve our dreams.

Thanks, Kate.

DIVA DIAMONDS

"Course, I expect to die at my zenith.
My star shall never set—I've sworn that too. And when that moment comes,
when I feel that I've done my best, my very best, I shall really die,
by my own hand some night at the end of the play. Onstage."

· · · ·

"I shouldn't like to go about swathed in furs unless they're sables.
I don't like anything cheap, particularly furs."

KATHARINE HEPBURN

AS EVA LOVELACE IN *MORNING GLORY*

GRAND HOTEL (1932)

STARS .... Greta Garbo, Wallace Beery,
.... John Barrymore, Lionel Barrymore, Joan Crawford

DIRECTOR .... Edmund Goulding

WRITER .... William A. Drake,
.... based on the play *Menschen im Hotel* by Vicki Baum

ACADEMY AWARDS .... Best Picture. No nominations for acting

· ·

Back when a good number of folks had nothing more than a piece of canvas to drape over themselves by way of shelter, thanks to the devastation of the Great Depression, *Grand Hotel* offered an opulent shelter from the storms of misfortune, and the reassuring message that even the mink-draped and top-hatted elite had their share of problems.

Amid the waterfall woodwork and marble floors of the Grand Hotel, one finds the beautiful people of Europe strutting through the lobby with their shoulders back and their necks stiff. But, ah, when they retire to their rooms . . . Scandals! Despair! Impending disaster! The business mogul (Wallace Beery) is desperate not to blow a deal, the wealthy baron (John Barrymore) has secretly lost his fortune and is terrified that he'll be found out, and the Russian ballerina (Greta Garbo) has some sort of traumatic heartbreak thing going on—it's kind of hard to tell with that St. Petersberg-by-way-of-Stockholm accent. While Beery and Barrymore fume and scheme, and Garbo keeps tossing herself onto couches and wailing about *v*anting to be alone and how she just couldn't go on stage tonight, she just couldn't, a couple of regular folks—a call girl

(Joan Crawford) and a dying accountant running through the last of his money (Lionel Barrymore)—finally get a little whiff of the champagne-and-caviar life. What follows are dramatic speeches about courage and danger, a crime and a shooting, and lots of gratuitous and well-lit profile shots that Greta Garbo and John Barrymore surely must have contracted for. And before the weekend is over, we experience hope and despair, birth and death, romance and passion, and enough dramatic thrashing about to make one wonder if any of these divas strained a muscle or two in their efforts to steal the show from their fellow performers.

When your own mundane problems have you in the doldrums and you're wishing for a dash of the luxurious life, tell 'em all that you *vant* to be alone. Then curl up with *Grand Hotel* and give yourself permission to emote to your heart's content.

GREAT LAST LINES IN OSCAR MOVIE HISTORY

"I've got to have more steps. I need more steps.
I've got to get higher . . . higher!"

WILLIAM POWELL
AS FLORENZ ZIEGFELD IN *THE GREAT ZIEGFELD*

INDEX

NANCY PESKE and BEVERLY WEST are best friends, identical cousins, and the coauthors of *Cinematherapy for the Soul: The Girl's Guide to Finding Inspiration One Movie at a Time, Cinematherapy for Lovers: The Girl's Guide to Finding True Love One Movie at a Time, Advanced Cinematherapy: The Girl's Guide to Finding Happiness One Movie at a Time, Cinematherapy: The Girl's Guide to Movies for Every Mood*, and *Bibliotherapy: The Girl's Guide to Books for Every Phase of Our Lives*. They live in New York City.